POWER MOVES

Bold Strategies from History's Most Innovative Leaders

FELIX GRAYSON

MINDSPARK
PUBLISHING

To the bold dreamers, fearless doers, and resilient leaders of yesterday, today, and tomorrow—this book is for you. May your vision inspire, your courage endure, and your legacy shape a better world.

"The future belongs to those who believe in the beauty of their dreams."

— *Eleanor Roosevelt*

ABOUT STONED PHILOSOPHER

Welcome to the *Stoned Philosopher* series—where timeless wisdom meets the modern world.

Each book distills powerful lessons from history's greatest minds, leaders, and thinkers— transforming their ideas into practical insights for today's challenges.

From mastering habits, calm, and resilience to understanding success, leadership, and meaning, this collection invites you to think deeper, live wiser, and see life from new perspectives.

Whether you're exploring *Modern Zen*, uncovering *The Wisdom of Warriors*, or seeking clarity through *The Art of Perspective*, every title offers a journey toward self-mastery and understanding.

Discover the full *Stoned Philosopher* collection and more at **FelixGrayson.com**, home of **Mind-Spark Publishing**—where knowledge, philosophy, and storytelling come together to spark lifelong curiosity.

FelixGrayson.com 🔍

Wisdom isn't something we find—it's something we grow into.

Let the journey begin.

CONTENTS

INTRODUCTION: THE CALL TO BOLD LEADERSHIP 10

CHAPTER 1: VISIONARY BEGINNINGS – CRAFTING A STRATEGY THAT INSPIRES 17

The Power of a Clear Vision 18

The Emotional Resonance of Vision 22

Crafting Long-Term Strategies 28

Inspiring Action Through Vision 34

CHAPTER 2: THE ART OF TIMING – KNOWING WHEN TO STRIKE 41

Recognizing the Right Moment 42

Patience vs. Urgency 48

Strategic Planning for Timing 54

Executing with Precision 61

CHAPTER 3: CALCULATED RISKS – BALANCING BOLDNESS AND CAUTION 68

The Anatomy of Risk-Taking 69

Learning from Failure 75

Risk Mitigation Strategies 81

Courage in Decision-Making 87

CHAPTER 4: NAVIGATING OPPOSITION – TURNING CHALLENGES INTO OPPORTUNITIES 94

Understanding Resistance 95

Strategic Conflict Resolution 101

Using Challenges to Innovate 107

The Growth Mindset 114

CHAPTER 5: COLLABORATION AND INFLUENCE – BUILDING A NETWORK OF ALLIES 121

The Importance of Relationships 122

Influence and Persuasion 128

Creating Synergistic Teams 133

Leveraging Collective Power 140

CHAPTER 6: ADAPTING TO CHANGE – INNOVATING IN THE FACE OF UNCERTAINTY 147

Recognizing the Need for Change 148

Agility in Leadership 154

Reframing Challenges as Opportunities 160

The Role of Resilience 166

CHAPTER 7: THE POWER OF EXECUTION – TURNING IDEAS INTO ACTION 173

Building Actionable Plans 174

Overcoming Execution Hurdles 179

The Discipline of Consistency 185

Measuring and Refining Success 191

CHAPTER 8: LEAVING A LEGACY – STRATEGIES THAT ENDURE BEYOND THEIR TIME 198

Defining an Enduring Legacy 199

Creating Systems for Sustainability 205

Mentorship and Succession 211

The Timelessness of Bold Strategies 217

CONCLUSION: THE POWER OF BOLD LEADERSHIP 224

INTRODUCTION: THE CALL TO BOLD LEADERSHIP

History remembers the bold. It celebrates those who dared to dream beyond their time, who transformed adversity into opportunity, and whose actions shaped not only their present but the future. Whether it's the visionary conquests of Alexander the Great, the enduring resilience of Nelson Mandela, or the transformative innovation of Steve Jobs, bold leadership has always been the force that propels humanity forward.

But bold leadership is not confined to history books or boardrooms. It is not the exclusive domain of rulers, revolutionaries, or entrepreneurs. Bold leadership exists within each of us. It begins with a decision—a choice to see the world not as it is but as it could be, and the courage to take the first step toward that vision.

This book is a guide for those who are ready to answer the call to bold leadership. Whether you are leading a team, a community, or simply striving to lead yourself with greater purpose, this journey is about uncovering the strategies, principles, and mindset that enable extraordinary leaders to make their mark.

The Power of Boldness

At its core, boldness is about possibility. It is the willingness to step into the unknown, to embrace uncertainty with confidence, and to act with conviction even when the path ahead is unclear. Bold leaders understand that every great achievement begins as an idea—a fragile spark that requires care, focus, and action to ignite into something transformative.

Consider the story of Henry Ford. In the early 20th century, the idea of making automobiles affordable to the average American was almost laughable. Cars were a luxury reserved for the wealthy, and the manufacturing process was slow and costly. But Ford saw a different future, one where mobility was accessible to all. His bold vision led to the creation of the assembly line, revolutionizing not only the automotive industry but modern manufacturing as a whole.

Ford's story is not just one of innovation but of determination. Bold leadership requires more than a vision—it demands the grit to overcome obstacles, the resilience to weather failure, and the adaptability to refine strategies when the unexpected arises.

A Timeless Journey

This book is not merely a recounting of history's greatest leaders; it is an exploration of timeless principles that transcend era, industry, and culture. From crafting a compelling vision to mastering the art of execution, from navigating opposition to leaving a legacy, the strategies presented here are as relevant today as they were in centuries past.

We draw lessons from the calculated risks of Elon Musk, the collaborative genius of Franklin D. Roosevelt, the creative empire-building of Walt Disney, and the moral courage of Martin Luther King Jr. These leaders faced vastly different challenges, yet their approaches reveal common threads—strategic thinking, emotional intelligence, and an unwavering commitment to their purpose.

As you read, you will notice that bold leadership is not about perfection. The leaders featured in these pages made mistakes, faced criticism, and encountered failure. But what set them apart was their ability to learn, adapt, and persist. They understood that leadership is not about avoiding challenges but about rising to meet them with clarity and resolve.

Why This Book Matters Now

The world today is a complex and rapidly changing landscape. From technological disruption to global crises, the need for bold leadership has never been more urgent. We are navigating a time where the status quo is no longer sufficient, where innovation and resilience are essential for progress.

This book is an invitation to see yourself as part of this narrative. You don't need to be a CEO, a political leader, or a historical figure to lead boldly. Leadership happens in classrooms, in families, in neighborhoods, and within ourselves. It is about how we choose to engage with the world, how we inspire others, and how we act on our values.

What You Will Discover

Throughout this book, you will explore eight chapters, each focusing on a critical aspect of bold leadership:

1. **Visionary Beginnings**: Learn how to craft a vision that inspires and mobilizes others, drawing from the strategies of history's most ambitious leaders.

2. **The Art of Timing**: Understand how to recognize the right moment to act, balancing patience with urgency.

3. **Calculated Risks**: Discover how to approach uncertainty with confidence, turning risks into opportunities.

4. **Navigating Opposition**: Develop strategies for turning challenges into catalysts for growth and innovation.

5. **Collaboration and Influence**: Build networks of allies and harness the power of collective

effort.

6. **Adapting to Change**: Embrace adaptability as a cornerstone of resilience and innovation.

7. **The Power of Execution**: Transform ideas into action through discipline, focus, and persistence.

8. **Leaving a Legacy**: Explore the timeless strategies that ensure your contributions endure beyond your lifetime.

Each chapter is designed to provide you with actionable insights, thought-provoking examples, and practical applications. The goal is not just to inform but to inspire—to equip you with the tools and mindset to lead boldly in your own life.

A Journey Worth Taking

As you embark on this journey, consider this: leadership is not about being extraordinary; it is about doing the extraordinary with the resources, opportunities, and challenges you have. It is about seeing beyond limitations, inspiring others to join you, and creating a positive ripple effect that extends far beyond your immediate actions.

The leaders we admire—past and present—did not start out as icons. They started as individuals with a vision, a purpose, and a willingness to act. Their stories remind us that bold leadership is not a destination but a process, one that is accessible to anyone willing to step forward.

This book is your companion on that process. It is a guide, a source of inspiration, and a call to action. Whether you are seeking to lead a movement, build a business, or navigate personal growth, the principles of bold leadership are yours to apply.

The future is shaped by those who dare to imagine it differently. By choosing to lead boldly, you join the ranks of those who refuse to settle for what is and strive instead for what could be. This is your moment to step into your potential, to embrace the challenges ahead, and to leave a mark that endures.

Let's begin.

CHAPTER 1: VISIONARY BEGINNINGS – CRAFTING A STRATEGY THAT INSPIRES

The Power of a Clear Vision

History has shown that the foundation of any extraordinary accomplishment begins with a clear and compelling vision. At its core, a vision is more than just an idea or a dream; it is a vivid picture of a desired future, one that ignites passion and directs purposeful action. Visionary leaders have an uncanny ability to distill complexity into clarity, articulating goals so bold and inspiring that they resonate across cultures and generations. This ability is not only a hallmark of great leadership but also a skill that can be cultivated and applied to any endeavor, no matter the scale.

One of the most striking examples of the power of vision is found in the story of Alexander the Great. Born into a world of fragmented city-states and warring kingdoms, Alexander dared to envision something unprecedented: the unification of the known world under one empire. From a young age, he was imbued with a sense of purpose, fueled by the teachings of Aristotle and the myths of Achilles. Yet, Alexander's greatness did not lie solely in his ambition; it was his ability to communicate his vision in a way that inspired unwavering loyalty among his followers.

When Alexander stood before his troops at the edge of the Hellespont, preparing to cross into Asia, he famously declared, "There is nothing impossible to him who will try." His vision of conquering the Persian Empire was not merely about territorial expansion; it was framed as a heroic mission to bring Greek culture and enlightenment to the world. This narrative gave his soldiers a sense of purpose far greater than their individual lives. It was this clarity of vision that sustained them through grueling campaigns, from the scorching deserts of Persia to the treacherous mountains of the Hindu Kush.

The power of a clear vision lies in its ability to unite people around a common goal. This principle transcends time, finding relevance in modern contexts as well. Consider Steve Jobs, the co-founder of Apple, whose vision for technology was not merely to create computers but to make tools that would "change the world." Jobs envisioned a future where technology was not confined to laboratories or offices but seamlessly integrated into everyday life. His famous declaration that Apple would "put a ding in the universe" encapsulated a bold and transformative vision, one that inspired both his team and the millions of users who embraced Apple's products.

Jobs' genius lay in his ability to simplify the complex. He understood that a clear vision must be communicated in a way that resonates emotionally. Whether unveiling the Macintosh in 1984 or introducing the iPhone in 2007, Jobs painted a picture of the future that was not only innovative but also deeply human. He spoke less about features and more about possibilities, less about technology and more about connection. In doing so, he turned his vision into a rallying cry, one that galvanized engineers, marketers, and customers alike.

For vision to be truly effective, it must do more than inspire; it must provide a roadmap for action. This is where clarity becomes indispensable. A well-articulated vision serves as a compass, guiding decisions and aligning efforts toward a shared destination. It helps individuals and teams navigate uncertainty, providing a sense of direction even in the face of challenges.

Yet, the creation of a clear vision is not without its challenges. It requires a leader to confront ambiguity and distill it into simplicity, a process that demands both intellectual rigor and emotional intelligence. Clarity does not mean oversimplification; rather, it is about cutting through the noise to articulate what truly matters. This is a skill that can be cultivated through reflection, dialogue, and a deep understanding of one's purpose.

The practical applications of this principle are manifold. Whether leading a team, starting a business, or pursuing personal growth, the ability to craft a clear vision is invaluable. Start by asking fundamental questions: What is the desired outcome? Why does it matter? How will it impact others? These questions help to refine a vision, ensuring it is both ambitious and grounded.

Once clarity is achieved, the next step is communication. A vision that lives only in the mind of its creator has no power. It must be shared, articulated in a way that ignites passion and builds consensus. This requires not only words but also actions that embody the vision, demonstrating commitment and authenticity.

As history shows, the power of a clear vision lies in its ability to transcend the individual and create a shared sense of purpose. Alexander the Great united disparate cultures under a single empire by framing his conquests as a mission of enlightenment. Steve Jobs revolutionized industries by envisioning a world where technology empowered humanity. Their examples remind us that vision is not merely a tool of leadership; it is a force that shapes the course of history.

In the end, the essence of a clear vision is its transformative potential. It begins with a single individual but has the power to inspire entire movements, build nations, and change the world. For those who aspire to lead with purpose and create lasting impact, the lesson is clear: vision is not just a starting point—it is the driving force behind every bold and innovative strategy.

The Emotional Resonance of Vision

A vision, no matter how clear, cannot move

mountains on its own. To truly inspire action, it must resonate deeply with the hearts and minds of others. This emotional resonance transforms a vision from a mere statement of intent into a powerful call to arms, igniting passion, loyalty, and collective effort. The leaders who achieve this do more than communicate ideas—they connect those ideas to the human experience, weaving them into the aspirations, struggles, and values of their audience.

One of the most iconic examples of this emotional resonance is Martin Luther King Jr.'s "I Have a Dream" speech. Delivered on the steps of the Lincoln Memorial during the 1963 March on Washington, this speech is remembered not just for its eloquence but for its ability to stir the soul. King did not merely outline a vision of racial equality; he painted a vivid picture of a future where his children would be judged not by the color of their skin but by the content of their character.

King's words were rooted in universal themes: freedom, justice, and hope. These themes transcended the specifics of the civil rights movement, appealing to the shared humanity of his audience. By tapping into the deeply held values of dignity and fairness, King's vision became not just a goal for activists but a moral imperative that resonated with millions. His deliberate use of repetition—"I have a dream"—created a rhythm that echoed the cadences of spiritual hymns, grounding his vision in both the cultural and emotional fabric of his listeners.

This emotional resonance is not limited to the grand oratory of social movements. It can be found in the corporate world, where leaders like Steve Jobs harnessed the same principles to inspire innovation. Jobs was a master of storytelling, understanding that products are not just objects but tools that fulfill human desires and aspirations. When unveiling the first iPhone in 2007, Jobs didn't focus on technical specifications. Instead, he described it as a device that would put "the power of the internet in your pocket," forever changing the way people connect with one another.

The brilliance of Jobs' presentations lay in their ability to evoke wonder and excitement. He framed Apple's innovations as more than technological advancements—they were gateways to a better life. By presenting his vision in terms of the emotional benefits to users, Jobs turned Apple's products into symbols of creativity, connection, and empowerment. This approach fostered an almost fanatical loyalty among customers, who felt not just like consumers but like participants in a shared journey of innovation.

The emotional resonance of a vision often comes from its ability to address the aspirations and fears of its audience. People are not motivated solely by logic or practicality; they are driven by their dreams, their struggles, and their longing for meaning. Great leaders understand this and craft their visions to align with these emotional undercurrents. They ask questions like: What do people hope to achieve? What are they afraid of losing? What stories do they tell themselves about who they are and who they want to become?

This connection to human emotion is not accidental—it is an intentional act of empathy. Empathy allows leaders to step into the shoes of their audience, understanding their experiences and speaking to their values. Abraham Lincoln exemplified this during his presidency, particularly in the Gettysburg Address. In just 272 words, Lincoln captured the grief and resolve of a nation torn apart by civil war, framing the Union's struggle as a test of the enduring value of democracy. His vision of "a new birth of freedom" resonated because it acknowledged the sacrifices of the past while offering hope for the future.

For contemporary readers, the lesson is clear: the most powerful visions are those that connect with people on a deeply human level. Crafting such a vision begins with listening—listening to the needs, fears, and aspirations of the individuals or communities you wish to inspire. It also requires vulnerability, as true emotional resonance often involves sharing one's own passions and convictions.

Practical applications of this principle abound, from leadership in organizations to personal relationships. For example, a manager looking to inspire a team might frame a project not as a task to be completed but as an opportunity to create something meaningful. By emphasizing how the work aligns with the team's values—whether it's innovation, collaboration, or impact—the manager can cultivate a sense of purpose that transcends mere deadlines and deliverables.

Similarly, in personal growth, crafting a vision for oneself can be an emotional exercise. Consider not just what you want to achieve but why it matters to you. Visualize the impact it will have on your life and the lives of those around you. This emotional connection to your goals can provide the motivation needed to persevere through challenges and setbacks.

At its heart, the emotional resonance of vision is about storytelling. Leaders like Martin Luther King Jr., Steve Jobs, and Abraham Lincoln understood that a vision is most compelling when it is woven into a narrative that reflects the shared experiences and values of its audience. A powerful vision tells a story of possibility, one that invites others to imagine themselves as protagonists in a journey toward something greater.

As we reflect on these examples, it becomes evident that the success of a vision is not determined solely by its content but by its ability to inspire and mobilize. When a vision resonates emotionally, it ceases to be just an idea; it becomes a movement, a mission, a legacy. For those seeking to lead with impact, the challenge is not just to articulate what you see but to connect it to the hopes and dreams of others, creating a shared vision that ignites the human spirit.

Crafting Long-Term Strategies

A compelling vision is the seed from which greatness grows, but without a long-term strategy, that vision is destined to wither. Long-term strategies act as the bridge between the dream and its realization, balancing ambition with the practical steps needed to achieve it. These strategies require a leader to think deeply about the future, anticipate obstacles, and create a roadmap that aligns bold objectives with realistic execution. History offers a treasure trove of examples where visionary leaders paired their aspirations with meticulously crafted strategies, none more striking than the Marshall Plan.

The Marshall Plan, officially known as the European Recovery Program, stands as a testament to the power of strategic foresight. In the aftermath of World War II, Europe was in ruins—economically, socially, and politically. The devastation was so severe that it threatened to destabilize the entire region, leaving it vulnerable to extremism and unrest. Recognizing this, U.S. Secretary of State George C. Marshall articulated a bold vision: to restore economic stability and foster cooperation among European nations, thereby securing peace and prosperity.

But this vision was not left to chance. The Marshall Plan was meticulously designed to address both immediate needs and long-term goals. It allocated over $13 billion in aid (equivalent to more than $100 billion today) to rebuild infrastructure, stimulate industry, and promote trade. The plan emphasized not just financial assistance but also the importance of collaboration among European countries, requiring them to work together to develop their own recovery strategies.

What made the Marshall Plan so effective was its balance of ambition and pragmatism. It aimed to achieve sweeping change—rebuilding an entire continent—yet it was grounded in actionable steps. It did not merely hand out aid but created a framework that incentivized self-reliance and cooperation. The result was a revitalized Europe that not only recovered but thrived, laying the groundwork for what would eventually become the European Union.

The principles behind the Marshall Plan can be applied to any long-term strategy. At its core was a deep understanding of the context in which it was implemented. Effective strategies begin with an honest assessment of the current state, identifying not only strengths and opportunities but also weaknesses and threats. This requires leaders to ask tough questions: What resources are available? What challenges are most pressing? What will success look like, and how can it be measured over time?

Crafting long-term strategies also demands the ability to balance flexibility with focus. Consider the approach taken by Mahatma Gandhi during India's struggle for independence. Gandhi's vision of a free and self-reliant India was unwavering, yet his strategies evolved in response to changing circumstances. When faced with British repression, Gandhi shifted tactics, from organizing nonviolent protests to promoting economic self-sufficiency through the use of indigenous goods. This adaptability ensured that his movement could withstand setbacks while remaining aligned with its ultimate goal.

Modern leaders can draw valuable lessons from these examples. One key takeaway is the importance of incremental progress. Long-term strategies are rarely executed in one sweeping motion; they unfold through a series of carefully planned and interconnected steps. This requires patience and a willingness to focus on small victories that build toward larger objectives. Each step serves as both a milestone and a learning opportunity, allowing leaders to refine their approach as they move forward.

Another critical element is communication. A strategy, no matter how well-crafted, cannot succeed if it is not understood and embraced by those tasked with executing it. Leaders must articulate their strategies clearly and consistently, ensuring that every stakeholder understands their role in the bigger picture. This requires not only clarity but also inspiration — connecting the day-to-day tasks to the broader vision, so that every action feels purposeful.

In addition to communication, successful strategies often hinge on the ability to anticipate and manage risks. This involves thinking several steps ahead, identifying potential obstacles, and developing contingency plans. A striking example of this is the Apollo program, which landed humans on the moon in 1969. The vision of putting a man on the moon was audacious, but NASA's strategy was painstakingly detailed. From testing rockets to simulating lunar landings, every possible failure scenario was considered and addressed. This meticulous planning allowed NASA to achieve what many had deemed impossible.

For individuals seeking to craft their own long-term strategies, the lessons are equally relevant. Whether building a career, starting a business, or pursuing personal growth, the key is to strike a balance between ambition and pragmatism. Begin by defining a clear goal and then break it down into manageable phases. For example, an entrepreneur might start with a vision of creating a globally recognized brand but focus first on establishing a strong local presence. Each phase should have specific objectives, timelines, and metrics for success, ensuring steady progress toward the ultimate goal.

Equally important is the willingness to adapt. No matter how well a strategy is planned, the future is inherently unpredictable. The ability to pivot in response to new information or unforeseen challenges is a hallmark of great leadership. This requires not only resilience but also humility—a recognition that strategies are tools, not dogmas, and that their value lies in their effectiveness, not their originality.

The final piece of the puzzle is alignment. Long-term strategies must align with the values and vision of the leader or organization. A strategy that achieves short-term gains at the expense of long-term integrity or purpose is ultimately self-defeating. Leaders must continually ask themselves whether their strategies reflect the core principles they wish to uphold, ensuring that every step forward is both meaningful and sustainable.

As the Marshall Plan, Gandhi's independence movement, and the Apollo program demonstrate, crafting long-term strategies is both an art and a science. It requires bold thinking tempered by practical action, a deep understanding of the present paired with a clear vision of the future. For those willing to embrace this challenge, the rewards are profound: the ability to turn even the most ambitious visions into enduring realities.

Inspiring Action Through Vision

A vision, no matter how bold or clear, ultimately holds little value if it remains confined to the realm of ideas. Its true power lies in its ability to inspire action, transforming aspirations into reality. The bridge between vision and action is built on the ability to mobilize others, to translate lofty goals into tangible steps, and to align efforts in pursuit of a shared purpose. The greatest leaders in history have excelled not only in envisioning a better future but also in rallying others to bring that future to life.

One of the most vivid illustrations of this principle is the leadership of Franklin D. Roosevelt during the New Deal era. When Roosevelt assumed the presidency in 1933, the United States was mired in the depths of the Great Depression. The economic collapse had eroded public trust, and despair was widespread. Roosevelt's vision for recovery was both ambitious and transformative, encompassing sweeping reforms in banking, labor, and social welfare. But it was not the vision alone that galvanized the nation—it was Roosevelt's ability to inspire collective action.

Roosevelt understood that his vision needed to resonate with the American people not just emotionally but practically. Through his "fireside chats," he spoke directly to the public, explaining complex policies in simple, relatable terms. He painted a picture of hope and resilience, framing the New Deal as a partnership between the government and the citizens. By emphasizing the role of every individual in the recovery effort, Roosevelt transformed passive observers into active participants. The result was a groundswell of support that enabled the implementation of programs like the Civilian Conservation Corps and the Works Progress Administration, which put millions of Americans to work.

The ability to mobilize action often hinges on a leader's skill in breaking down grand visions into actionable steps. Visionaries like Mahatma Gandhi understood this intuitively. Gandhi's dream of an independent India was monumental in scope, yet his strategies for achieving it were rooted in simple, replicable acts of resistance. The Salt March of 1930 is a powerful example of this. By leading a 240-mile march to protest the British monopoly on salt production, Gandhi transformed an abstract struggle for independence into a concrete, relatable action. This single act of defiance not only galvanized Indians across the subcontinent but also drew international attention to the cause, highlighting the oppressive nature of British rule.

The genius of Gandhi's approach lay in its accessibility. He empowered ordinary people to take part in the movement, showing them that even small actions, when multiplied across a population, could have profound effects. This principle remains as relevant today as it was in Gandhi's time. Whether leading a social movement or managing a team, the ability to translate vision into achievable actions is a cornerstone of effective leadership.

Inspiring action also requires the creation of a

shared sense of purpose. People are motivated not just by what they are doing but by why they are doing it. Simon Sinek, in his influential work *Start with Why*, emphasizes that the most successful leaders and organizations are those that clearly articulate their purpose. By connecting individual actions to a larger mission, leaders can inspire commitment and perseverance, even in the face of challenges.

Consider the story of Elon Musk and his vision for SpaceX. Musk's goal of making humanity a multiplanetary species is audacious, yet it is his ability to inspire his team and the public that has driven the company's remarkable achievements. Musk frames his work not merely as building rockets but as safeguarding the future of humanity. This purpose infuses every project with meaning, attracting some of the brightest minds in engineering and inspiring a level of dedication that transcends the typical workplace. By aligning his vision with a cause that resonates on a global scale, Musk has mobilized not just a company but an entire industry.

For leaders seeking to inspire action, authenticity is paramount. A vision that is disconnected from the leader's values or actions will ring hollow, undermining trust and engagement. Authentic leaders lead by example, demonstrating their commitment to the vision through their own behavior. This was exemplified by Nelson Mandela during his presidency in South Africa. Mandela's vision of reconciliation and unity was not just a political goal; it was a deeply personal mission shaped by his 27 years of imprisonment. His willingness to forgive his oppressors and work toward a united South Africa inspired others to do the same, creating a foundation for the country's transition from apartheid to democracy.

Another critical component of mobilizing action is fostering a culture of collaboration. Leaders cannot achieve their vision alone; they must inspire others to contribute their talents and resources. This requires not only clarity of purpose but also an environment that values inclusivity and innovation. During the Apollo program, NASA exemplified this principle by bringing together experts from diverse fields to tackle the unprecedented challenge of landing a man on the moon. The success of the mission was not solely the result of technological advances but also the collective effort of thousands of individuals united by a shared goal.

Practical application of these lessons begins with clear communication. Leaders must articulate not only what they aim to achieve but also how each individual's contributions will make a difference. This can be achieved through storytelling, one of the most powerful tools for inspiring action. Stories have the ability to connect abstract ideas to real-world experiences, making them relatable and memorable. Whether recounting past successes, sharing personal experiences, or envisioning future possibilities, storytelling allows leaders to bridge the gap between vision and action.

Ultimately, inspiring action through vision is about creating momentum. It starts with small, intentional steps that build confidence and credibility. Each success reinforces the belief in the vision, generating the energy needed to tackle larger challenges. This process is iterative, requiring leaders to continually refine their approach and adapt to new circumstances.

The leaders who excel in this domain are those

who understand that vision is not a solitary pursuit but a collective journey. They recognize that the true measure of leadership is not in the scope of their ideas but in their ability to inspire others to act on them. From Franklin D. Roosevelt to Elon Musk, the greatest visionaries have shown us that the power of a vision lies not in its articulation but in its realization.

For those who aspire to lead with impact, the message is clear: vision is the spark, but action is the flame. To inspire action is to transform potential into progress, dreams into reality, and ideas into lasting change.

CHAPTER 2: THE ART OF TIMING – KNOWING WHEN TO STRIKE

Recognizing the Right Moment

Timing, as the adage goes, is everything. In the world of leadership and strategy, the ability to recognize the right moment can mean the difference between triumph and failure. This skill is not just about acting quickly or decisively—it is about sensing when conditions align to create a unique window of opportunity. Great leaders possess an almost instinctual grasp of timing, honed through experience, observation, and an acute understanding of their environment. History is rich with examples of leaders who mastered this art, none more famously than Napoleon Bonaparte.

Napoleon's military genius was rooted not only in his tactical brilliance but also in his unparalleled sense of timing. He understood that even the most well-conceived plan could falter if executed at the wrong moment. One of his most celebrated campaigns, the Battle of Austerlitz in 1805, demonstrates how timing can transform a precarious situation into a decisive victory.

Facing the combined forces of Russia and Austria, Napoleon appeared to be at a disadvantage. His troops were outnumbered, and the terrain seemed to favor the enemy. However, Napoleon recognized that his opponents were eager to exploit what they perceived as his vulnerability. He deliberately feigned weakness, retreating strategically and abandoning elevated positions to lure the enemy into overextending themselves.

On the morning of the battle, fog blanketed the field, obscuring visibility. Napoleon seized the moment, waiting until the sun burned away the mist to launch his attack. The timing was impeccable: the enemy forces were disorganized and poorly positioned, their momentum disrupted by the conditions Napoleon had engineered. What followed was a masterclass in precision and timing, as Napoleon's forces executed a series of maneuvers that shattered the coalition army. The victory at Austerlitz not only solidified Napoleon's reputation but also demonstrated how recognizing the right moment can amplify the impact of a strategy.

The ability to sense the right moment is not confined to military contexts. It is a universal skill, applicable to business, politics, and personal decision-making. Consider the story of Oprah Winfrey, who built her media empire by mastering the art of timing. In the late 1980s, talk shows were a crowded and competitive space, with hosts like Phil Donahue dominating the airwaves. Oprah recognized that the cultural zeitgeist was shifting, and audiences were craving something more personal and authentic.

Rather than mimicking her competitors, Oprah introduced a format that emphasized emotional connection and self-discovery. She knew when to ask probing questions and when to allow silence to deepen the impact of a guest's story. Her intuitive sense of timing extended beyond the television set, as she carefully chose when to launch new ventures, from her book club to her production company. By aligning her actions with the evolving desires of her audience, Oprah not only differentiated herself but also redefined an entire industry.

The challenge of recognizing the right moment lies in its subtlety. It requires a deep awareness of context, a sensitivity to shifts in circumstances, and the ability to anticipate the ripple effects of a decision. Leaders who excel in this area often display a blend of analytical and intuitive thinking. They gather information, assess patterns, and weigh probabilities, but they also trust their instincts when the moment arrives.

For Napoleon, this meant understanding the psychological tendencies of his enemies and leveraging their overconfidence. For Oprah, it meant tuning into the emotional needs of her audience and responding with authenticity. In both cases, timing was not an isolated decision but a culmination of careful preparation and acute perception.

Practical applications of this principle abound in modern contexts. In the business world, recognizing the right moment can mean identifying when to enter a market, launch a product, or pivot a strategy. Companies like Netflix have demonstrated this with remarkable success. In the early 2000s, as DVD rentals dominated the home entertainment industry, Netflix sensed the gradual shift toward digital streaming. While competitors clung to traditional models, Netflix invested heavily in streaming technology, timing their transition perfectly to capitalize on the rise of broadband internet. This decision not only disrupted the industry but also positioned Netflix as a global leader in entertainment.

For individuals, the ability to recognize the right moment often comes down to cultivating patience and awareness. It means resisting the urge to act prematurely, even when the pressure to move is intense. This is where philosophical reflection can offer guidance. The ancient Stoics, for example, emphasized the importance of aligning one's actions with the natural flow of events. Marcus Aurelius wrote, "Observe how all things are born from change; teach yourself to wait and to discern the right moment for action." This mindset encourages a balance between readiness and restraint, allowing individuals to act decisively when the time is right.

To develop this skill, one must first cultivate observation. Pay attention to the dynamics of your environment, whether it is the behavior of competitors, the mood of a market, or the patterns of your own life. Look for signals that indicate change—shifts in trends, emerging opportunities, or the resolution of uncertainties. These signals often reveal the moments when action is most likely to succeed.

Second, practice patience. Timing is not just about seizing opportunities but also about waiting for them. This requires the discipline to hold back when conditions are not yet favorable, trusting that preparation will meet opportunity in due course. Warren Buffett, one of the world's most successful investors, exemplifies this principle. Buffett's strategy involves waiting for "fat pitch" opportunities—those rare moments when the odds are overwhelmingly in his favor. His patience has allowed him to avoid impulsive decisions and achieve extraordinary long-term success.

Finally, embrace adaptability. Recognizing the right moment often involves navigating uncertainty and adjusting plans as new information emerges. Flexibility allows leaders to pivot when conditions change, ensuring that their timing remains aligned with reality. This dynamic approach to timing is what separates reactive leaders from proactive visionaries.

Ultimately, the art of recognizing the right moment is a combination of preparation, observation, and intuition. It is about understanding not just what needs to be done but when it must be done to achieve maximum impact. Leaders like Napoleon, Oprah, and Warren Buffett remind us that timing is not a passive act of waiting but an active process of engagement with the world.

For those who seek to lead with purpose and effectiveness, the lesson is clear: timing is not just a tool—it is a force multiplier. When combined with a clear vision and thoughtful strategy, the ability to act at the right moment can turn ordinary efforts into extraordinary achievements.

Patience vs. Urgency

Timing, as a cornerstone of success, often demands the delicate art of balancing patience and urgency. Leaders who excel in this domain demonstrate an ability to assess when waiting is prudent and when decisive action is imperative. While these two approaches might appear to be in opposition, they are, in fact, complementary forces, each vital in its own context. History offers striking examples of how mastery over this dynamic can lead to extraordinary outcomes, from Warren Buffett's deliberate investment strategies to the swift and unrelenting Blitzkrieg tactics of World War II.

Patience, often seen as a passive virtue, is in reality an active and intentional practice. It is not simply the act of waiting but of preparing, observing, and positioning oneself to act at the optimal moment. Warren Buffett, one of the most successful investors in history, exemplifies the power of patience in the high-stakes world of finance. Buffett's investment philosophy, rooted in the teachings of Benjamin Graham, emphasizes the importance of identifying "fat pitch" opportunities—rare moments when the odds of success are overwhelmingly in one's favor.

Buffett's career is marked by his ability to resist impulsive decisions, even when markets are volatile or trends are tempting. Instead, he waits for undervalued assets that align with his criteria for long-term growth. His approach, famously described as "buying wonderful companies at fair prices," is a testament to his belief that patience is not merely a virtue but a competitive advantage. By waiting for the right opportunities, Buffett has consistently achieved remarkable returns while avoiding the pitfalls of speculative behavior.

The discipline of patience is not confined to investing. It is a universal principle that applies to leadership, strategy, and personal growth. Patience allows leaders to gather information, build resources, and refine their plans, ensuring that their actions are both deliberate and impactful. It also fosters resilience, enabling individuals to endure setbacks without losing sight of their goals.

However, patience without action can lead to stagnation. This is where the counterbalance of urgency becomes essential. Urgency is the ability to recognize when immediate action is necessary to seize an opportunity or avert a crisis. It is characterized by speed, decisiveness, and a willingness to take calculated risks. Few historical examples illustrate this better than the Blitzkrieg tactics employed by Nazi Germany during the early years of World War II.

Blitzkrieg, or "lightning war," was a military strategy designed to achieve swift and over-whelming victories through the rapid deployment of forces. It relied on a combination of speed, surprise, and coordination, allowing the German army to outmaneuver and overwhelm their adversaries. In 1940, during the invasion of France, the Blitzkrieg approach enabled German forces to bypass the heavily fortified Maginot Line and achieve a stunning victory in just six weeks.

While the ethical implications of Blitzkrieg tactics are deeply troubling, the strategic principles behind them underscore the power of urgency. By acting decisively and exploiting their enemies' unpreparedness, German commanders were able to achieve objectives that would have been impossible through slower, more conventional methods. The effectiveness of these tactics lay in their timing—striking quickly before opponents could organize a coherent response.

The contrast between Buffett's patience and the Blitzkrieg's urgency highlights the dual nature of timing. Patience allows for careful preparation and the accumulation of advantages, while urgency enables leaders to capitalize on fleeting opportunities. The key to success lies in understanding when each approach is appropriate.

For leaders, the decision to act with patience or urgency often hinges on the context. In stable environments, patience can be a powerful ally, providing the space to plan meticulously and build sustainable systems. Conversely, in volatile or high-pressure situations, urgency may be necessary to address immediate challenges or prevent catastrophic losses.

Practical applications of this balance are evident in modern business strategy. Startups, for example, often operate in a state of urgency, racing to secure funding, launch products, and capture market share before competitors. Yet, as these companies mature, they must transition to a more patient approach, focusing on long-term growth and stability. The ability to navigate this shift is often the difference between success and failure.

This duality is also present in personal decision-making. Consider the pursuit of a career goal. Patience might involve investing in education, gaining experience, and building a network, all of which lay the groundwork for future opportunities. But when a rare job opening arises or a pivotal meeting occurs, urgency becomes critical. The ability to act swiftly and decisively in such moments can turn years of preparation into tangible success.

The philosophical underpinnings of this balance can be found in the works of thinkers like Sun Tzu and the Stoics. Sun Tzu, in *The Art of War*, emphasizes the importance of timing, advising leaders to "strike when the iron is hot" but to wait for the right conditions before doing so. Similarly, the Stoics advocate for measured action, encouraging individuals to align their efforts with the natural flow of events. This philosophy underscores the idea that patience and urgency are not mutually exclusive but part of a continuum.

For those seeking to cultivate this balance, self-awareness is essential. Leaders must understand their own tendencies and biases, recognizing whether they are more inclined toward patience or urgency. By developing the capacity to shift between these modes as circumstances demand, they can make more effective decisions.

Another critical factor is situational awareness. Leaders must remain attuned to the dynamics of their environment, identifying signals that indicate when conditions are ripe for action or when it is wiser to wait. This requires a combination of analytical skills, emotional intelligence, and intuition.

Ultimately, the interplay between patience and urgency is a dance—a dynamic process that evolves with time and context. Leaders who master this balance are not only more effective but also more adaptable, capable of thriving in a wide range of situations. Warren Buffett's investment patience and the Blitzkrieg's decisive urgency may seem worlds apart, but they share a common thread: an acute awareness of timing and a relentless commitment to aligning action with opportunity.

For those who aspire to lead with impact, the lesson is clear. Patience and urgency are not opposing forces but complementary tools. By understanding when to wait and when to strike, leaders can harness the full power of timing, turning challenges into opportunities and vision into reality.

Strategic Planning for Timing

Great decisions rarely happen by accident. While intuition and spontaneity can play a role in leadership, the most impactful choices are often the result of meticulous planning. Strategic planning for timing involves creating a framework that allows leaders to anticipate the right moments for action. This process blends analytical tools, historical insights, and a refined sense of intuition, enabling leaders to navigate complex environments with precision and confidence.

History offers countless examples of how strategic planning has been used to master the art of timing. One of the most instructive is the Allied invasion of Normandy during World War II, known as D-Day. The success of this operation hinged not only on military might but also on the careful orchestration of timing. The Allies faced the daunting challenge of launching a massive amphibious assault against a well-fortified enemy. Success would depend on synchronizing countless variables, from weather conditions to troop movements.

The planning process for D-Day began years

before the actual invasion, involving exhaustive analysis and preparation. Meteorological data played a critical role, as the invasion required specific weather conditions: clear skies for air support, calm seas for landing craft, and a low tide to expose German defenses. Allied meteorologists monitored weather patterns for months, ultimately identifying a narrow window on June 6, 1944, when conditions would be ideal.

Timing was also crucial in misleading the Germans. The Allies launched an elaborate deception campaign, Operation Fortitude, to convince the enemy that the invasion would occur elsewhere. By carefully orchestrating the flow of information and coordinating false troop movements, they ensured that German forces were spread thin when the real assault began.

The lessons of D-Day highlight the importance of using data-driven predictions to anticipate the right moment for action. Modern leaders can apply similar principles in a variety of contexts. For example, businesses often rely on market research and predictive analytics to determine the optimal timing for product launches. By analyzing consumer behavior, competitive trends, and economic indicators, companies can identify when their offerings are most likely to succeed.

However, data alone is not enough. Strategic planning also requires the ability to synthesize information into actionable insights. This is where intuition, shaped by experience and context, comes into play. Consider the leadership of Steve Jobs, who had an uncanny ability to sense when the market was ready for groundbreaking innovations. While Apple undoubtedly used market research, Jobs' timing often seemed to stem from an intuitive understanding of cultural and technological shifts.

The release of the iPod in 2001 is a prime example. At the time, digital music was still a niche market, and portable MP3 players were clunky and uninspiring. Jobs recognized that the convergence of factors—improved storage technology, increasing internet speeds, and the growing popularity of digital music—created an opportunity for a game-changing product. His intuition was supported by Apple's meticulous planning, from the seamless integration of the iPod with iTunes to its sleek and user-friendly design.

Jobs' ability to balance data-driven analysis with intuition reflects a broader truth about strategic planning: timing is as much an art as it is a science. Leaders must be willing to embrace uncertainty and trust their instincts, even when the data is incomplete. This requires a mindset of curiosity and adaptability, as well as a commitment to continuous learning.

Another critical aspect of strategic planning for timing is scenario analysis. This involves envisioning multiple possible outcomes and preparing for each one. The Apollo 11 mission to the moon exemplifies this approach. NASA's engineers and astronauts spent years rehearsing every aspect of the mission, simulating potential problems and devising solutions. This exhaustive preparation ensured that when unforeseen challenges arose—such as the need for a manual landing adjustment due to boulder-strewn terrain—Neil Armstrong and Buzz Aldrin were equipped to respond effectively.

In today's fast-paced world, scenario analysis is a valuable tool for leaders across industries.

By considering a range of possibilities, from best-case scenarios to worst-case contingencies, leaders can make more informed decisions and reduce the risk of being caught off guard. This approach fosters resilience and enables organizations to pivot quickly when conditions change.

Strategic planning for timing also benefits from collaboration. The most successful leaders recognize that they cannot anticipate every variable on their own. They surround themselves with diverse teams, drawing on a wide range of perspectives and expertise. This collaborative approach not only enhances the quality of planning but also builds buy-in among stakeholders, ensuring that everyone is aligned and prepared to act when the time comes.

Philosophically, strategic planning for timing aligns with the concept of kairos, an ancient Greek term that refers to the opportune moment for action. Unlike chronos, which measures linear time, kairos emphasizes the qualitative aspects of timing—the ability to discern when the conditions are right to achieve a specific goal. This concept reminds us that timing is not just about precision but also about perspective. It requires leaders to step back, assess the broader context, and align their actions with the natural flow of events.

For contemporary leaders, the practical applications of this principle are vast. Whether managing a team, launching a campaign, or navigating a career, the ability to plan strategically for timing can yield significant advantages. Start by identifying key milestones and defining what success looks like at each stage. Use data and intuition to anticipate challenges and opportunities, and create contingency plans to address uncertainties.

Equally important is the willingness to adjust the plan as circumstances evolve. Strategic planning is not a static process; it is dynamic and iterative, requiring constant refinement. Leaders who embrace this flexibility are better equipped to seize opportunities and navigate obstacles, ensuring that their timing remains aligned with their goals.

Ultimately, strategic planning for timing is about creating a foundation for informed action. It combines the rigor of analysis with the creativity of intuition, the precision of data with the adaptability of human insight. Leaders who master this process are not only better prepared to recognize the right moment but also more capable of shaping it, turning potential into progress and vision into reality.

Executing with Precision

Timing is the art of knowing when to act, but execution is the discipline of ensuring that the action is carried out with precision. It is in this intersection of timing and execution that success is forged. The greatest leaders in history have demonstrated that even the most well-timed decision can falter without careful implementation. Conversely, precise execution can elevate a well-timed decision into a transformative moment. A compelling example of this balance can be found in John F. Kennedy's handling of the Cuban Missile Crisis in October 1962, a period often regarded as the closest the world has ever come to nuclear war.

The Cuban Missile Crisis began when American intelligence discovered Soviet missile installations under construction in Cuba, just 90 miles from U.S. shores. The stakes were existential: allowing the missiles to become operational would shift the balance of power in the Cold War, while a rash response risked escalating into a full-scale nuclear conflict. The situation demanded not only swift action but also extraordinary precision in decision-making and execution.

Kennedy's approach was marked by his ability to navigate the crisis with measured resolve. His first step was to impose a naval "quarantine" on Cuba, a term carefully chosen to avoid the connotations of aggression associated with a blockade. This action sent a clear message to the Soviet Union without provoking immediate retaliation. Simultaneously, Kennedy maintained open channels of communication with Soviet Premier Nikita Khrushchev, using backchannel diplomacy to explore avenues for de-escalation.

The precision of Kennedy's execution lay in his ability to manage both the immediate threat and the long-term implications of his decisions. He resisted pressure from his military advisors to launch an airstrike, recognizing that such an action could spiral into a broader conflict. Instead, he chose a strategy that combined firmness with flexibility, giving Khrushchev a face-saving way to withdraw the missiles. The resolution of the crisis, which involved the Soviets dismantling their installations in exchange for a U.S. pledge not to invade Cuba, was a masterclass in executing a well-timed decision with precision.

The lessons from the Cuban Missile Crisis extend far beyond geopolitics. At its core, the episode illustrates the importance of aligning execution with both immediate goals and broader objectives. Leaders must be attuned to the ripple effects of their actions, ensuring that the way a decision is implemented supports its intended outcomes.

In the business world, the ability to execute with precision is often what separates successful ventures from failed ones. Consider Amazon's decision to launch Prime, its membership-based service, in 2005. The timing was critical: e-commerce was growing rapidly, and competitors were beginning to challenge Amazon's dominance. However, it was not just the idea of a membership program that made Prime a success—it was the flawless execution of the concept.

Amazon invested heavily in logistics and technology to ensure that the promise of two-day shipping could be consistently fulfilled. The company also used data analytics to tailor its offerings, creating a seamless and personalized experience for customers. The launch of Prime was not just a timely decision; it was a meticulously executed strategy that transformed customer expectations and reshaped the retail industry.

Executing with precision requires a combination of clarity, coordination, and commitment. Clarity ensures that every stakeholder understands their role and how it aligns with the larger vision. This is particularly important in complex initiatives, where miscommunication or ambiguity can lead to costly errors.

Coordination involves orchestrating multiple moving parts to achieve a unified outcome. This often requires leaders to act as integrators, ensuring that resources, people, and processes are aligned. In the case of Kennedy, this meant balancing the demands of his military advisors, diplomats, and allies while maintaining control over the narrative presented to the public.

Commitment, meanwhile, is the willingness to see an action through to its conclusion, even when challenges arise. Precision is not a one-time effort; it requires ongoing vigilance and adaptability. Leaders must be prepared to refine their approach in response to feedback or changing circumstances, ensuring that the execution remains aligned with the desired outcome.

Philosophically, the concept of executing with precision resonates with the teachings of Confucius, who emphasized the importance of aligning one's actions with ethical principles and practical realities. Confucius taught that effective leadership requires a deep understanding of both the means and the ends, ensuring that the methods used to achieve a goal are as honorable as the goal itself. This perspective underscores the idea that how something is done is as important as what is done.

For contemporary leaders, the practical applications of this principle are manifold. In project management, for example, executing with precision often involves defining clear objectives, setting realistic timelines, and monitoring progress through key performance indicators. These practices ensure that every aspect of a project is aligned with its overarching goals.

In personal development, precision can take the form of setting specific, measurable goals and developing a structured plan to achieve them. For instance, someone pursuing a fitness goal might track their progress through metrics such as weight, strength, or endurance, adjusting their routine based on the results. This level of precision not only increases the likelihood of success but also builds confidence and momentum.

The ability to execute with precision is particularly valuable in times of uncertainty. When faced with ambiguity, leaders who can maintain clarity and focus are better equipped to navigate challenges and seize opportunities. This requires a mindset of continuous improvement, where each action is viewed as a learning opportunity.

Ultimately, the power of execution lies in its

ability to transform vision into reality. As the Cuban Missile Crisis and Amazon's Prime launch demonstrate, the way a decision is implemented can have far-reaching consequences, shaping not only immediate outcomes but also long-term trajectories. Leaders who master the art of executing with precision are not only more effective but also more impactful, leaving a legacy of excellence and achievement.

For those who aspire to lead with purpose, the lesson is clear: timing sets the stage, but execution brings the performance to life. By combining well-timed decisions with precise and deliberate actions, leaders can achieve results that resonate far beyond the moment, creating a lasting impact on their organizations, communities, and the world.

CHAPTER 3: CALCULATED RISKS – BALANCING BOLDNESS AND CAUTION

The Anatomy of Risk-Taking

Risk-taking is an integral part of leadership and innovation, yet it is also one of the most misunderstood aspects of strategy. While boldness and courage are often celebrated, successful leaders understand that not all risks are created equal. A calculated risk is one that balances ambition with analysis, daring with discernment. It is not about gambling blindly but about making informed decisions that align with both opportunity and purpose. This art of measured risk-taking is exemplified by figures like Elon Musk and Queen Elizabeth I, whose ventures and gambits reveal the principles that distinguish calculated risks from reckless ones.

Elon Musk, a modern icon of innovation, has built his career on ventures that many deemed impossibly risky. From the outset, his journey was marked by bold leaps into uncharted territory. Musk's vision to revolutionize space travel through SpaceX, for example, was audacious in both scope and execution. At a time when private companies were scarcely considered viable players in the aerospace industry, Musk bet not just his fortune but his reputation on the idea that reusable rockets could transform humanity's access to space.

However, Musk's approach was far from reckless. What set SpaceX apart was the meticulous planning and relentless pursuit of feasibility that underpinned its ambition. Musk surrounded himself with some of the brightest minds in engineering, leveraging their expertise to create innovative designs that reduced costs while enhancing performance. He also prepared for failure, knowing that success in such a high-stakes field would require multiple iterations and substantial setbacks.

The early years of SpaceX were fraught with challenges, including three consecutive failed launches. For many, this would have been the end of the road. But Musk's calculated approach meant he had contingency plans in place. He had allocated resources to ensure one final launch attempt, which succeeded spectacularly. This balance of boldness and preparation is what defines a calculated risk: the willingness to pursue a high-stakes opportunity tempered by a commitment to manage and mitigate potential losses.

Queen Elizabeth I provides an equally compelling historical example. Her reign was characterized by political instability, economic challenges,
and the constant threat of invasion. Yet, Elizabeth navigated these dangers with a strategic
brilliance that often involved taking calculated
risks. One of the most famous instances was her
decision to support the English fleet against the
Spanish Armada in 1588.

At the time, Spain was the dominant naval power,
and its armada was considered invincible. Elizabeth faced immense pressure to negotiate or
concede, as an outright confrontation seemed
doomed to fail. However, she recognized that
inaction carried its own risks, potentially em-
boldening Spain and eroding England's sover-
eignty.

Elizabeth's decision to fight was not made light-
ly. She invested in naval innovations, including
smaller, faster ships that could outmaneuver
the larger Spanish galleons. She also relied
on intelligence networks to anticipate Spain's
movements, giving the English fleet a strategic
advantage. Furthermore, Elizabeth's charismat-

ic leadership played a crucial role in rallying her forces. Her famous speech at Tilbury, where she declared, "I have the body of a weak and feeble woman, but I have the heart and stomach of a king," galvanized her troops and bolstered morale.

The defeat of the Spanish Armada was a turning point in history, establishing England as a rising power and securing Elizabeth's legacy. Yet, it was not a gamble—it was a calculated risk that balanced the necessity of action with a thoughtful assessment of the odds.

Both Musk and Elizabeth demonstrate that calculated risks are not about eliminating uncertainty but about managing it. This involves several key principles. First, it requires a clear understanding of the stakes. What is to be gained, and what is to be lost? For Musk, the potential reward was nothing less than revolutionizing space travel; for Elizabeth, it was the preservation of her nation's independence.

Second, calculated risks involve thorough preparation. This means gathering information, analyzing scenarios, and building contingencies.

Musk's engineering teams and Elizabeth's naval innovations were not afterthoughts — they were integral to their strategies.

Third, successful risk-taking demands decisiveness. Leaders must be willing to act when the moment arises, even if the path is fraught with uncertainty. This decisiveness is often rooted in confidence, not just in the outcome but in one's ability to adapt and respond to challenges as they emerge.

For contemporary readers, the lessons from these examples are both timeless and actionable. In business, taking calculated risks might involve launching a new product, entering an emerging market, or adopting disruptive technologies. The key is to balance boldness with preparation, ensuring that risks are not just ambitious but also informed.

In personal growth, calculated risks often take the form of pursuing opportunities that stretch one's comfort zone. This might mean changing careers, starting a business, or moving to a new city. The same principles apply: understand the stakes, prepare for challenges, and commit fully to the decision.

Philosophically, the concept of calculated risk-taking aligns with the teachings of Aristotle, who emphasized the importance of the "golden mean" — the balance between extremes. Courage, Aristotle argued, is not the absence of fear but the ability to act appropriately in the face of fear. Calculated risks embody this balance, combining the audacity to dream big with the prudence to plan wisely.

The anatomy of risk-taking is ultimately about embracing uncertainty while maintaining control. It is about recognizing that every meaningful endeavor carries an element of danger but also understanding that with the right approach, those dangers can be navigated. Elon Musk's ventures and Queen Elizabeth I's political gambits remind us that the most remarkable achievements often lie on the other side of risk — not reckless risk, but risks that are calculated, deliberate, and aligned with a greater purpose.

For leaders and individuals alike, the challenge is not to avoid risk but to master it. By learning to balance boldness with caution, preparation with decisiveness, and ambition with realism, we can transform uncertainty into opportunity and possibility into achievement.

Learning from Failure

Failure is an inevitable companion on the journey of risk-taking, but it is also one of the most powerful teachers. For those bold enough to embrace risk, setbacks are not the end of the road — they are stepping stones toward eventual success. Leaders who learn from failure are able to refine their strategies, sharpen their skills, and build the resilience needed to persevere. History is filled with examples of innovators and visionaries who faced repeated failures, yet their willingness to adapt and learn transformed those setbacks into the foundation for extraordinary achievements.

One of the most compelling stories of learning from failure is that of the Wright brothers, Wilbur and Orville, who pioneered human flight. In the late 19th and early 20th centuries, the idea of powered flight was more fantasy than reality. Numerous inventors had tried and failed, often with disastrous results. The Wright brothers, however, approached the challenge with a unique combination of ambition, curiosity, and a willingness to fail forward.

The early years of their experimentation were marked by setbacks. Their initial gliders often crashed, and their designs frequently fell short of achieving sustained flight. These failures, while frustrating, were not viewed as insurmountable obstacles. Instead, they became opportunities for the brothers to learn and improve. Each unsuccessful test flight provided valuable data, revealing flaws in their designs and helping them understand the complex interplay of aerodynamics, lift, and propulsion.

What set the Wright brothers apart was their scientific rigor and tenacity. They meticulously documented their experiments, analyzing the results to refine their theories. When existing data on aerodynamics proved unreliable, they built their own wind tunnel to test various wing shapes. Their iterative approach to problem-solving was a masterclass in learning from failure: every setback was a lesson, every crash a step closer to success.

In December 1903, after years of relentless experimentation, the Wright brothers achieved the first controlled, sustained flight of a powered aircraft. This historic moment was not the result of a single breakthrough but the culmination of countless small adjustments and lessons learned from failure. Their story underscores a profound truth: failure is not the opposite of success — it is an integral part of the process.

The ability to learn from failure is not limited to technological innovation; it is a universal skill that applies to all domains of leadership. Consider the story of J.K. Rowling, the author of the *Harry Potter* series. Before becoming one of the most successful writers of all time, Rowling faced repeated rejections from publishers. Her manuscript was turned down by twelve publishing houses, each of which doubted the commercial viability of her story.

Rather than giving up, Rowling used the feedback from these rejections to improve her manuscript. She refined her pitch, adjusted her approach, and persisted in submitting her work. When Bloomsbury finally accepted *Harry Potter and the Philosopher's Stone*, it became clear that her perseverance had paid off. Rowling's experience illustrates that failure is not a verdict—it is a test of one's determination and adaptability.

Philosophically, the concept of learning from failure aligns with the principles of Stoicism, which teaches that setbacks are opportunities for growth. Marcus Aurelius, one of the most famous Stoic philosophers, wrote, "The impediment to action advances action. What stands in the way becomes the way." This mindset encourages individuals to view challenges not as barriers but as catalysts for improvement.

In the modern world, the ability to learn from failure is increasingly recognized as a critical component of success. Companies like Google and Amazon have built cultures that embrace experimentation and encourage employees to take risks. Google's "moonshot" projects, such as self-driving cars and internet balloons, are designed with the understanding that many will fail. The company's leadership views these failures not as losses but as valuable learning experiences that drive innovation.

Similarly, Amazon's founder Jeff Bezos has

often spoken about the importance of failure in the company's growth. From the early struggles of the Kindle to the flop of the Fire Phone, Amazon has experienced its share of setbacks. Yet, each failure has provided insights that have informed the company's successes, such as the development of Amazon Web Services and the dominance of its e-commerce platform.

For individuals, learning from failure involves cultivating a mindset of curiosity and resilience. Start by reframing setbacks as opportunities for growth. When faced with a failure, ask yourself: What went wrong? What can I learn from this experience? How can I apply these lessons moving forward? This reflective approach allows you to extract value from every challenge, transforming disappointment into progress.

Another key aspect of learning from failure is maintaining perspective. It is easy to become discouraged when faced with setbacks, but it is important to remember that failure is a natural part of any ambitious endeavor. Even the most successful leaders and innovators have faced moments of doubt and defeat. What sets them apart is their ability to persevere and adapt.

Building a support network can also make a significant difference. Surround yourself with mentors, peers, and allies who can provide guidance, encouragement, and constructive feedback. These relationships can help you navigate the challenges of risk-taking and provide valuable insights when things don't go as planned.

Ultimately, the lessons of the Wright brothers, J.K. Rowling, and countless others remind us that failure is not a destination—it is a journey. It is a process of trial and error, of testing boundaries and pushing limits. For those willing to embrace failure as a teacher, the rewards can be transformative.

The act of learning from failure is not just about recovering from setbacks; it is about building a foundation for future success. It is about developing the resilience to face uncertainty, the humility to acknowledge mistakes, and the wisdom to grow stronger with each challenge. As history shows, the path to greatness is rarely a straight line—but for those who persevere, it is a path worth taking.

Risk Mitigation Strategies

Taking calculated risks is essential for growth and innovation, but even the most carefully considered risks come with potential downsides. The ability to minimize those downsides while maximizing the chance of success is what separates reckless gambles from strategic decisions. Effective risk mitigation doesn't eliminate risk entirely—such a goal is often unrealistic—but it reduces uncertainty to a manageable level. By employing tools like scenario planning, resource allocation, and contingency development, leaders can approach challenges with confidence, knowing they are prepared for a range of outcomes.

One of the most celebrated historical examples of risk mitigation is the Apollo program, NASA's ambitious effort to land humans on the moon. The stakes were astronomical—scientifically, politically, and financially. Failure would not only have represented a monumental loss of resources but also a blow to national morale during the height of the Cold War. To mitigate these risks, NASA employed an unparalleled level of planning, innovation, and preparation.

Central to NASA's strategy was scenario planning, a tool that involves envisioning multiple potential outcomes and preparing for each. For the Apollo missions, this meant anticipating everything from minor technical glitches to catastrophic failures. NASA engineers devised extensive simulations, testing spacecraft systems under extreme conditions to identify and address vulnerabilities. Astronauts trained relentlessly for a variety of contingencies, from equipment malfunctions to emergency landings.

This thorough preparation paid off during the Apollo 11 mission in 1969. When Neil Armstrong and Buzz Aldrin approached the lunar surface, they encountered a navigation error that placed their module off-course, directly above a boulder-strewn area. Armstrong, drawing on his training and the flexibility built into the mission plan, manually piloted the lander to a safe spot. The mission's success was a testament to the power of risk mitigation: while unforeseen challenges arose, they had been anticipated, and the team was equipped to respond effectively.

Scenario planning is not limited to space exploration; it is a vital tool in business and leadership. One modern example is Toyota, which has long been praised for its ability to manage risk through strategic foresight. The company employs a practice known as "pre-mortem analysis," where teams imagine that a project has failed and then work backward to identify potential causes. This proactive approach allows Toyota to address vulnerabilities before they become problems, enhancing the company's resilience and adaptability.

Another critical component of risk mitigation is resource allocation. Leaders must ensure that sufficient resources—whether financial, human, or technological—are devoted to managing potential risks. This principle was exemplified during World War II by the Allied forces' planning for D-Day. The invasion of Normandy was an audacious gamble, requiring the coordination of hundreds of thousands of troops, thousands of vehicles, and vast quantities of supplies.

To mitigate the risks of such a massive operation, the Allies invested heavily in logistical planning. This included stockpiling resources, developing specialized equipment like amphibious landing craft, and establishing supply chains that could sustain the invasion forces. The success of D-Day was not guaranteed, but the meticulous allocation of resources ensured that the troops had the support they needed to overcome formidable obstacles.

Resource allocation is equally important in business. Companies that fail to invest adequately in risk management often find themselves unprepared when challenges arise. Conversely, those that allocate resources strategically can turn risks into opportunities. Amazon, for example, has consistently invested in infrastructure and technology to support its rapid expansion. By building a robust logistics network and embracing automation, the company has mitigated risks associated with scaling while maintaining its competitive edge.

Contingency planning is another essential element of risk mitigation. While scenario planning focuses on anticipating a range of possibilities, contingency planning involves creating specific, actionable plans for addressing worst-case scenarios. A famous example of contingency planning can be found in the leadership of Winston

Churchill during World War II.

Churchill recognized that the war's outcome hinged on the resilience of the British people and the ability to sustain the fight under adverse conditions. To prepare for the possibility of a German invasion, Churchill oversaw the development of a national network of defenses, including coastal fortifications and guerrilla resistance units. These measures were never fully tested, as the invasion never materialized, but their existence bolstered morale and ensured that Britain was prepared for the worst.

For contemporary leaders, the principles of contingency planning are highly applicable. Whether managing a project, launching a product, or navigating a crisis, having a clear plan for worst-case scenarios provides a safety net. It also fosters confidence among stakeholders, who are reassured by the knowledge that potential risks have been accounted for.

Risk mitigation strategies are not just about avoiding failure—they are about creating conditions for success. By reducing uncertainty, leaders can focus their energy and resources on seizing opportunities rather than reacting to crises. This proactive approach aligns with the teachings of Sun Tzu, who wrote in *The Art of War*: "The skillful fighter puts himself into a position which makes defeat impossible, and does not miss the moment for defeating the enemy." This philosophy emphasizes the importance of preparation and positioning, ensuring that risks are managed without compromising the ability to act boldly.

Practical applications of risk mitigation extend beyond organizations to individuals. For instance, someone pursuing a major life change, such as starting a business or moving to a new city, can employ these principles. Scenario planning might involve considering different financial or career outcomes, resource allocation might include saving money or building a support network, and contingency planning could address potential setbacks, such as a delayed opportunity or unexpected expenses.

Ultimately, the goal of risk mitigation is not to eliminate risk but to ensure that risks are taken intelligently. By combining foresight, preparation, and adaptability, leaders can navigate uncertainty with confidence. The stories of NASA, Toyota, the Allied forces, and countless others remind us that even the most daunting challenges can be managed with the right strategies.

For those who aspire to lead with purpose, the message is clear: risk is an inherent part of growth and innovation, but it does not have to be paralyzing. With effective risk mitigation, leaders can embrace uncertainty, take bold actions, and achieve outcomes that once seemed impossible.

Courage in Decision-Making

Courage is the invisible force that empowers leaders to make decisions in the face of uncertainty. It is not the absence of fear but the ability to act despite it. In high-stakes situations, where outcomes are unpredictable and the stakes are high, courage becomes the defining trait of effective leadership. This courage is not impulsive or reckless; it is thoughtful, grounded in purpose, and tempered by an awareness of risk. It allows leaders to embrace uncertainty and take bold action, even when the path ahead is unclear.

One of the most iconic demonstrations of courage in decision-making is the story of Abraham Lincoln's issuance of the Emancipation Proclamation during the American Civil War. By 1862, the war had reached a critical juncture. The Union had suffered significant losses, and public morale was wavering. Lincoln faced mounting pressure to end the conflict, but he also recognized that the war's ultimate purpose needed to transcend mere political or territorial preservation. For Lincoln, the abolition of slavery was not just a moral imperative but a strategic necessity to redefine the Union's cause and weaken the Confederacy's economic foundation.

The decision to issue the Emancipation Proclamation was fraught with risk. Lincoln knew it could alienate border states that were loyal to the Union but still permitted slavery. He also faced opposition from within his own party and skepticism from the public, many of whom doubted the practicality of such a move. Yet, Lincoln understood that decisive action was needed to change the trajectory of the war and the course of history.

Lincoln's courage lay not only in making the

proclamation but also in the calculated timing of its announcement. He waited for a Union victory—the Battle of Antietam—to lend credibility to the proclamation and ensure it was perceived as a position of strength rather than desperation. When the Emancipation Proclamation took effect on January 1, 1863, it transformed the Civil War into a moral crusade, bolstering support for the Union both domestically and internationally.

This example illustrates that courage in decision-making is not about acting rashly; it is about aligning one's actions with deeply held principles, even in the face of opposition and uncertainty. It is about understanding that true leadership often requires stepping into the unknown, guided by a commitment to a greater purpose.

The need for courage in decision-making extends beyond historical moments to everyday leadership. In the business world, leaders often face decisions that carry significant risks, from launching new products to entering untested markets. Howard Schultz, the former CEO of Starbucks, demonstrated this kind of courage when he made the controversial decision to expand Starbucks globally.

In the early 1990s, Schultz envisioned Starbucks as a global brand, a move that many critics considered overly ambitious and financially risky. At the time, coffee culture outside North America was less established, and the idea of charging premium prices for coffee in emerging markets seemed implausible. Schultz, however, had a clear vision: Starbucks was not just selling coffee—it was selling an experience.

Schultz's courage to act boldly was rooted in his belief in the company's mission and the meticulous planning that supported his vision. He personally visited potential markets, studying consumer behavior and identifying cultural nuances that could shape the Starbucks experience. When the company opened its first international store in Tokyo in 1996, it became an instant success, proving that Schultz's bold decision was well-founded. Today, Starbucks operates in over 80 countries, a testament to the power of courageous decision-making.

Courage in decision-making often requires a willingness to challenge the status quo. Leaders who dare to think differently and take unconventional paths are the ones who drive innovation and change. This principle aligns with the teachings of philosopher Søren Kierkegaard, who argued that true courage involves a "leap of faith" — the act of stepping into the unknown with conviction.

For individuals, embracing courage in decision-making begins with developing a mindset of resilience and adaptability. Start by acknowledging that fear is a natural response to uncertainty, but it does not have to dictate your actions. Instead, use fear as a signal to prepare, reflect, and assess the potential risks and rewards of a decision.

It is also essential to cultivate self-awareness. Understanding your values and priorities provides a foundation for courageous action. When your decisions are aligned with your core beliefs, it becomes easier to overcome doubt and resistance. This alignment not only strengthens your resolve but also inspires confidence in those who follow your lead.

Another critical element of courage in decision-making is embracing vulnerability. Leaders who are open about the challenges they face and the risks they take build trust and credibility. This openness fosters collaboration and encourages others to contribute their insights and expertise, enhancing the quality of decisions.

Practical applications of courage in decision-making are abundant. For example, a leader managing a struggling project might need the courage to pivot or even abandon the initiative, despite sunk costs or external pressures. Similarly, an entrepreneur might decide to launch a bold new venture, knowing that failure is a possibility but also recognizing the potential for transformative success.

In personal growth, courage might involve making life-altering decisions, such as changing careers, pursuing a long-held passion, or confronting difficult truths. These decisions often require stepping out of your comfort zone and embracing the uncertainty that comes with change.

Ultimately, courage in decision-making is about recognizing that every choice carries risk, but not every risk is worth avoiding. It is about understanding that growth and progress are born from the willingness to face uncertainty and act with conviction. Abraham Lincoln, Howard Schultz, and countless other leaders remind us that courage is not just a quality—it is a practice, one that can be cultivated through self-awareness, preparation, and a commitment to purpose.

For those who aspire to lead with impact, the lesson is clear: courage is the bridge between vision and action, the force that transforms intention into reality. By embracing uncertainty and acting boldly, leaders can inspire others, overcome challenges, and create lasting change in their organizations, communities, and lives.

CHAPTER 4: NAVIGATING OPPOSITION – TURNING CHALLENGES INTO OPPORTUNITIES

Understanding Resistance

Resistance is an inescapable element of leadership and innovation. Whenever bold ideas challenge the status quo, they inevitably encounter opposition, whether from competitors, entrenched systems, or societal norms. While resistance can be frustrating, it also offers a unique opportunity for growth, adaptation, and transformation. To navigate opposition effectively, leaders must first understand its sources and dynamics. History is replete with examples of individuals who turned resistance into a catalyst for progress, none more vividly than Mahatma Gandhi and Nikola Tesla.

Gandhi's campaign for India's independence from British colonial rule epitomizes the ability to understand and harness resistance. The British Empire, at its height, represented a seemingly insurmountable force. Its authority was reinforced by legal, economic, and military structures designed to suppress dissent and maintain control. Yet, Gandhi recognized that these systems, formidable as they were, relied on the cooperation and compliance of the people they governed.

Instead of confronting the British with violence, Gandhi chose a path of nonviolent resistance, or satyagraha. This strategy was not merely a moral stance; it was a deeply pragmatic approach rooted in an understanding of power dynamics. Gandhi's campaigns, such as the Salt March of 1930, highlighted the injustices of British policies while mobilizing millions of Indians to participate in acts of civil disobedience. By refusing to pay taxes, boycott British goods, and defy colonial laws, ordinary citizens disrupted the mechanisms of colonial rule, forcing the British to confront the untenability of their position.

Gandhi's genius lay in his ability to see opposition not as an obstacle but as a mirror. Resistance, he understood, often reveals the vulnerabilities of those in power. By exposing the moral contradictions of British rule—professing ideals of liberty and justice while denying them to Indians—Gandhi undermined the legitimacy of the Empire in the eyes of the world. This approach not only rallied internal support but also galvanized international opinion, paving the way for India's eventual independence.

Understanding resistance also requires acknowledging its complexity. Opposition is rarely monolithic; it arises from a combination of fears, interests, and values. Gandhi's approach worked because he addressed these layers. He appealed to the conscience of the British people while empowering Indians to reclaim their agency. By understanding the motivations of both his adversaries and his allies, Gandhi was able to craft a strategy that transcended confrontation and fostered transformation.

In a vastly different context, Nikola Tesla faced resistance of a more technical and commercial nature. Tesla, a visionary inventor, was one of the key figures in the development of alternating current (AC) electricity. His revolutionary ideas clashed with the entrenched interests of Thomas Edison, who championed direct current (DC) systems. The "War of the Currents," as it came to be known, was not just a battle of technologies but a clash of visions for the future of electricity.

Edison, backed by powerful financial interests, launched a smear campaign against AC, portraying it as dangerous and unreliable. Tesla, by contrast, focused on demonstrating the superiority of his system through practical applications. Collaborating with industrialist George Westinghouse, Tesla showcased the potential of AC at the 1893 World's Columbian Exposition in Chicago, where the entire fair was illuminated using his technology. This public demonstration not only countered the narrative of AC's dangers but also positioned it as the future of electrical power.

Tesla's ability to navigate resistance stemmed from his deep understanding of both the technical and human aspects of opposition. He recognized that Edison's campaign was as much about protecting investments as it was about technological merit. By proving AC's practicality and safety, Tesla shifted the conversation from fear to possibility, ultimately securing its adoption as the global standard for electricity.

The experiences of Gandhi and Tesla highlight several key insights into understanding resistance. First, opposition often arises from fear — fear of change, fear of loss, or fear of the unknown. Leaders who acknowledge and address these fears, rather than dismissing them, are better equipped to navigate resistance. Gandhi's appeals to morality and Tesla's emphasis on safety both addressed the underlying anxieties of their adversaries, diffusing hostility and building credibility.

Second, resistance is often rooted in vested interests. Those who benefit from the status quo have a natural incentive to resist change. This dynamic can be seen in industries ranging from energy to technology, where established players often push back against disruptive innovations. Understanding these interests allows leaders to anticipate and counteract opposition, whether through negotiation, demonstration, or coalition-building.

Finally, resistance can be a source of valuable feedback. Opposition forces leaders to refine their ideas, strengthen their arguments, and address potential weaknesses. Tesla's battle with Edison compelled him to develop more robust demonstrations of AC's superiority, while Gandhi's campaigns were continually shaped by the challenges he encountered. By viewing resistance as a dialogue rather than a deadlock, leaders can use it to enhance their strategies and achieve more impactful outcomes.

For contemporary leaders, understanding resistance begins with active listening. Pay attention to the concerns and motivations of those who oppose you, whether they are competitors, stakeholders, or societal forces. This requires a willingness to engage in honest conversations and a commitment to empathy, even when faced with hostility.

It also involves cultivating patience and persistence. Resistance is rarely overcome overnight; it requires sustained effort and adaptability. Leaders must be prepared to iterate their approaches, learning from each encounter and adjusting their strategies accordingly.

Philosophically, the concept of understanding resistance aligns with the teachings of Lao Tzu, who wrote in the *Tao Te Ching*: "The soft overcomes the hard; the slow overcomes the fast." This principle emphasizes the power of subtlety and flexibility in addressing opposition, reminding us that resistance is often best met with understanding rather than force.

Ultimately, resistance is not something to be feared or avoided. It is a natural response to change and a vital part of any transformative process. By understanding its sources and dynamics, leaders can navigate opposition with clarity and purpose, turning challenges into opportunities for growth.

The stories of Gandhi and Tesla remind us that opposition, while daunting, is also a mirror—a reflection of the values, fears, and aspirations that shape our world. For those who seek to lead with impact, the challenge is not to eliminate resistance but to understand it, harness it, and use it as a force for progress.

Strategic Conflict Resolution

Conflict is an inevitable part of leadership, yet it is often in the resolution of conflict that the greatest opportunities arise. Strategic conflict resolution is not about avoiding disagreements or suppressing dissent but about transforming adversarial relationships into collaborative ones. It requires leaders to approach conflicts with empathy, creativity, and a willingness to find common ground. By employing techniques such as diplomacy and negotiation, leaders can turn adversaries into allies, fostering solutions that benefit all parties involved.

One of the most celebrated examples of strategic conflict resolution is the leadership of Nelson Mandela during South Africa's transition from apartheid to democracy. Mandela inherited a nation deeply divided along racial and economic lines, with decades of institutionalized oppression fostering mistrust and resentment on all sides. The challenge of uniting South Africa required not only political vision but also the ability to engage with opponents who had long viewed one another as irreconcilable enemies.

Mandela's approach was rooted in empathy and an unshakable belief in the power of dialogue. Instead of seeking revenge against the architects of apartheid, Mandela extended an olive branch, recognizing that the future of South Africa depended on reconciliation. He worked tirelessly to build trust with white leaders, including former President F.W. de Klerk, while also addressing the grievances of the Black majority.

A cornerstone of Mandela's strategy was the Truth and Reconciliation Commission (TRC), a platform that allowed victims and perpetrators of apartheid-era crimes to share their experiences. The TRC was not about erasing the past but about acknowledging it, creating a foundation for healing and mutual understanding. This process of open dialogue helped South Africa move forward without descending into the cycle of retribution that has plagued many post-conflict societies.

Mandela's success illustrates the transformative potential of diplomacy. By focusing on shared goals—such as peace, stability, and economic growth—he was able to transcend the divisions of the past and build a coalition for the future. His leadership demonstrates that effective conflict resolution is not about "winning" the argument but about creating a win-win outcome that aligns with the broader vision.

In a vastly different context, the Cuban Missile Crisis of 1962 provides another compelling example of strategic conflict resolution. For thirteen days, the United States and the Soviet Union teetered on the brink of nuclear war, with each side unwilling to back down. President John F. Kennedy faced intense pressure from his advisors, many of whom advocated for a military strike against the Soviet missile sites in Cuba.

Instead of escalating the conflict, Kennedy chose a path of negotiation. Through backchannel diplomacy, he and Soviet Premier Nikita Khrushchev engaged in a delicate exchange of proposals, seeking a resolution that would allow both sides to de-escalate without losing face. The eventual agreement—whereby the Soviets removed their missiles from Cuba in exchange for a U.S. pledge not to invade Cuba and the removal of American missiles from Turkey—was a masterstroke of negotiation. It averted war while preserving the dignity of both nations.

Kennedy's handling of the crisis underscores the importance of patience and perspective in conflict resolution. By resisting the urge to act impulsively, he created the space for dialogue and compromise. His approach highlights a key principle of negotiation: the ability to see the situation through the eyes of one's adversary and address their underlying concerns.

The lessons from Mandela and Kennedy are as relevant today as they were in their time. Strategic conflict resolution begins with understanding the motivations and fears of all parties involved. This requires active listening, empathy, and a commitment to finding common ground. Leaders who approach conflicts with humility and openness are better positioned to identify solutions that satisfy the interests of all stakeholders.

Another critical aspect of conflict resolution is the ability to reframe the narrative. When adversaries are entrenched in opposing positions, it can be helpful to shift the focus from the problem to the potential for collaboration. For example, instead of framing a negotiation as a battle over limited resources, leaders can highlight the opportunity to create value through partnership. This approach not only reduces tension but also fosters a sense of shared purpose.

In the business world, strategic conflict resolution can be seen in the rise of collaborative ventures between former rivals. One notable example is the partnership between Apple and IBM, two companies that spent decades competing in the personal computing market. In 2014, the two tech giants announced a strategic alliance to develop enterprise solutions for mobile devices. By setting aside their differences and focusing on their complementary strengths, Apple and IBM were able to create innovative products that benefited both companies and their customers.

For individuals, strategic conflict resolution is a valuable skill in both professional and personal contexts. Whether navigating workplace disagreements or resolving disputes in personal relationships, the ability to approach conflicts constructively can lead to stronger connections and better outcomes. Start by acknowledging the perspectives of others and seeking to understand their concerns. This requires a willingness to set aside ego and focus on the larger picture.

Philosophically, the principles of conflict resolution align with the teachings of the Buddha, who emphasized the importance of compassion and understanding in resolving disputes. The Buddha taught that anger and hostility only perpetuate suffering, while empathy and dialogue create the conditions for peace. This wisdom reminds us that conflict is not an end in itself but an opportunity for growth and transformation.

Ultimately, strategic conflict resolution is about turning challenges into opportunities. By engaging with adversaries in a spirit of collaboration, leaders can transform opposition into support, creating solutions that advance their vision and strengthen their communities. The stories of Mandela, Kennedy, and countless others remind us that even the most intractable conflicts can be resolved with patience, empathy, and creativity.

For those who aspire to lead with impact, the lesson is clear: conflict is not something to be feared or avoided but something to be embraced as a chance to learn, grow, and create meaningful change. By approaching conflicts with a strategic mindset, leaders can navigate even the most challenging situations and emerge stronger, wiser, and more effective.

Using Challenges to Innovate

Opposition and resistance often seem like barriers to success, but they can also serve as catalysts for innovation and resilience. When faced with challenges, individuals and organizations are forced to think differently, adapt to changing circumstances, and create new solutions. The process of overcoming resistance often drives breakthroughs, transforming what might initially appear as setbacks into opportunities for growth. Few stories illustrate this principle more vividly than the resurgence of Apple under Steve Jobs.

By the mid-1990s, Apple was struggling to survive. Once a trailblazer in personal computing, the company had lost its way, producing a fragmented product lineup and falling far behind its competitors. Jobs, who had co-founded Apple in 1976 but was ousted in 1985, returned to the company in 1997 during one of its darkest hours. Apple was nearing bankruptcy, its stock was plummeting, and industry analysts doubted its ability to recover.

Jobs inherited a company riddled with resistance, both internally and externally. Internally, Apple's culture was fractured, with divisions between teams and a lack of clear direction. Externally, the company faced stiff competition from Microsoft, which had established dominance with its Windows operating system. Additionally, Apple's reputation had suffered, with many consumers and critics perceiving its products as overpriced and outmoded.

Rather than being deterred by these challenges, Jobs embraced them as opportunities to rethink Apple's approach. One of his first moves was to simplify the company's product line, focusing on a core set of innovative and beautifully designed products. This decision was not without resistance, as it involved cutting existing product lines and shifting resources toward untested ideas. Jobs believed, however, that focusing on fewer, better products would allow Apple to regain its identity and stand out in a crowded market.

This strategy culminated in the launch of the iMac in 1998, a product that not only revitalized Apple's image but also redefined personal computing. The iMac's sleek design, vibrant colors, and user-friendly interface set it apart from the beige boxes that dominated the market. Its success demonstrated that innovation was not just about technology but also about how products connect with people.

Jobs's ability to use resistance as a springboard for innovation reached new heights with the introduction of the iPod in 2001. At the time, the market for digital music players was fragmented, and piracy was rampant. The challenge of creating a device that could appeal to consumers while addressing industry concerns was daunting. Yet, Jobs saw an opportunity to redefine how people experienced music.

The iPod was more than just a device—it was part of an ecosystem that included iTunes, a platform for purchasing and managing music legally. By addressing the concerns of both consumers and record labels, Apple transformed the music industry, proving that innovation often involves finding solutions that bridge competing interests.

Jobs's tenure at Apple highlights a key principle: challenges force leaders to question assumptions and explore uncharted territory. The resistance Apple faced—whether from skeptical consumers, entrenched competitors, or internal divisions—provided the impetus for the company to reinvent itself.

The idea that challenges drive innovation is not limited to Apple. History is replete with examples of how resistance has fostered creativity and resilience. During World War II, for instance, the scarcity of resources led to a wave of technological advancements, from radar systems to synthetic materials. These innovations not only contributed to the war effort but also had lasting impacts on civilian industries.

The process of using challenges to innovate often begins with a shift in perspective. Instead of viewing resistance as a problem to be avoided, leaders can see it as a source of valuable information. Opposition reveals pain points, unmet needs, and opportunities for improvement. By engaging with resistance, leaders gain insights that can inform their strategies and inspire new ideas.

For example, when Howard Schultz took over Starbucks in the 1980s, he faced significant resistance to his vision of turning the company into a global brand. Many stakeholders doubted the viability of expanding Starbucks beyond its core market, arguing that Schultz's emphasis on creating a "third place" between home and work was overly idealistic. Rather than backing down, Schultz used this skepticism to refine his vision, focusing on customer experience and product quality. Today, Starbucks is a global phenomenon, with Schultz's vision at its heart.

Another critical aspect of using challenges to innovate is fostering a culture of experimentation. Organizations that embrace experimentation are more likely to develop creative solutions, as they are not constrained by fear of failure. Google's "20% time," a policy that allows employees to spend a portion of their workweek on passion projects, has resulted in innovations like Gmail and Google Maps. By encouraging employees to explore new ideas, Google has turned challenges into opportunities for growth.

Philosophically, the concept of using challenges to innovate aligns with the teachings of Friedrich Nietzsche, who famously said, "What does not kill me makes me stronger." This perspective emphasizes the transformative power of adversity, suggesting that resistance can lead to growth and self-discovery.

For contemporary leaders, the practical applications of this principle are manifold. When
faced with resistance, start by analyzing its root
causes. What are the underlying fears, concerns,
or motivations driving opposition? Use this
information to identify opportunities for innovation, whether by addressing unmet needs,
resolving pain points, or challenging outdated
assumptions.

Next, foster an environment that encourages
creative thinking. This involves giving teams
the freedom to experiment, fail, and learn. Recognize that breakthroughs often come from
unexpected places, and be willing to explore
unconventional solutions.

Finally, cultivate resilience. Innovation is rarely
a linear process; it involves setbacks, iterations,
and moments of doubt. Leaders who persevere
through resistance are more likely to achieve
lasting success.

Ultimately, the ability to use challenges to innovate is a hallmark of great leadership. Steve
Jobs's reinvention of Apple, Howard Schultz's

transformation of Starbucks, and countless other examples demonstrate that resistance is not a barrier but a stepping stone. By embracing opposition as an opportunity for creativity and growth, leaders can turn challenges into triumphs, forging a path toward greater impact and success.

The Growth Mindset

In the face of opposition and adversity, one's perspective can make all the difference. The concept of a growth mindset—popularized by psychologist Carol Dweck—posits that individuals and organizations thrive when they view challenges as opportunities to learn, adapt, and evolve. This mindset fosters resilience, encourages innovation, and transforms setbacks into stepping stones for success. Few companies embody the power of the growth mindset more than Amazon, which has consistently leveraged challenges to drive personal and organizational growth.

When Jeff Bezos founded Amazon in 1994, the company was a small online bookstore operating in a rapidly changing digital landscape.

From the outset, Amazon faced skepticism from industry insiders who doubted the viability of e-commerce. Traditional retailers dominated the market, and many dismissed the internet as a passing fad. However, Bezos embraced these challenges with a growth mindset, seeing them not as barriers but as opportunities to disrupt the status quo.

One of the defining moments in Amazon's journey was its decision to expand beyond books and become the "everything store." This shift required enormous investment, both financially and strategically. Critics questioned Amazon's ability to manage such a broad inventory, and the company faced logistical challenges that would have deterred most leaders. Yet, Bezos saw these obstacles as opportunities to innovate.

Rather than sticking to conventional methods, Amazon pioneered solutions that redefined the retail industry. Its development of advanced algorithms for product recommendations, investment in warehouse automation, and commitment to fast delivery were all responses to the challenges of scaling. These innovations were not just reactive; they reflected a proactive mindset that sought to turn adversity into competitive advantage.

The introduction of Amazon Prime in 2005 is a prime example of this approach. At the time, the concept of offering unlimited free shipping for a flat annual fee seemed risky, particularly given the costs involved. However, Bezos viewed Prime as an investment in customer loyalty. By addressing a common pain point—shipping costs—Amazon not only differentiated itself from competitors but also created a model that encouraged repeat business. Prime's success, which has since expanded to include streaming services, exclusive deals, and more, demonstrates how a growth mindset can transform a challenge into a game-changing opportunity.

The principles that drive Amazon's growth mindset are deeply rooted in its culture. Bezos has often emphasized the importance of being "stubborn on vision, flexible on details." This philosophy encapsulates the essence of the growth mindset: a clear commitment to long-term goals combined with the adaptability to navigate short-term challenges. It encourages employees to experiment, learn from failures, and continuously refine their approaches.

Beyond Amazon, the growth mindset has played a pivotal role in many historical and contemporary success stories. Consider Thomas Edison, whose journey to invent the light bulb involved over a thousand failed experiments. When asked about these failures, Edison famously replied, "I have not failed. I've just found 10,000 ways that won't work." This perspective reflects the core of the growth mindset: an unwavering belief that each setback is a step closer to success.

Similarly, in the world of sports, Michael Jordan's legendary career was fueled by a growth mindset. Known for his unparalleled work ethic and relentless pursuit of excellence, Jordan often credited his failures for shaping his success. "I've missed more than 9,000 shots in my career," he once said. "I've lost almost 300 games. Twenty-six times, I've been trusted to take the game-winning shot and missed. I've failed over and over and over again in my life. And that is why I succeed."

The growth mindset is not only about learning from failure but also about embracing change.

In a rapidly evolving world, those who resist change risk stagnation, while those who adapt thrive. This principle is evident in Amazon's ability to expand into diverse industries, from cloud computing with Amazon Web Services (AWS) to entertainment with Amazon Studios. Each new venture has brought its own set of challenges, but the company's willingness to experiment and learn has allowed it to lead in multiple domains.

For leaders and organizations seeking to cultivate a growth mindset, the first step is to create an environment that encourages curiosity and resilience. This involves celebrating effort and progress, rather than focusing solely on outcomes. By reframing mistakes as learning opportunities, leaders can foster a culture where employees feel empowered to take risks and innovate.

Philosophically, the growth mindset aligns with the teachings of stoicism, particularly the idea that obstacles are opportunities. Marcus Aurelius, the Roman emperor and Stoic philosopher, wrote in his *Meditations*: "The impediment to action advances action. What stands in the way becomes the way." This perspective encourages individuals to embrace challenges as essential to growth, transforming adversity into a source of strength.

On a personal level, adopting a growth mindset involves shifting how we perceive our abilities and potential. Instead of viewing talent as fixed, recognize that skills and intelligence can be developed through effort and perseverance. This mindset not only enhances performance but also builds resilience, as individuals learn to approach setbacks with optimism and determination.

The growth mindset also applies to leadership. Leaders who embody this mindset inspire their teams to push boundaries and embrace change. They model humility by acknowledging their own limitations and a willingness to learn, creating a culture of continuous improvement.

In practical terms, the growth mindset can be cultivated through reflection and feedback. Take time to analyze challenges and setbacks, asking questions like: What did I learn from this experience? How can I apply these lessons moving forward? Encourage open communication within teams, creating opportunities for dialogue and collaboration.

Ultimately, the growth mindset is about embracing the journey of becoming—not just as individuals but as organizations and communities. The stories of Amazon, Edison, and Jordan remind us that challenges are not roadblocks but stepping stones. For those who aspire to lead with impact, the lesson is clear: growth is not a destination; it is a process. By adopting a mindset of curiosity, resilience, and adaptability, we can turn obstacles into opportunities and unlock our fullest potential.

CHAPTER 5: COLLABORATION AND INFLUENCE – BUILDING A NETWORK OF ALLIES

The Importance of Relationships

At the heart of effective leadership lies the ability to build and sustain meaningful relationships. Leadership is not a solitary endeavor—it is a collective journey shaped by the people we align with and the networks we cultivate. Throughout history, alliances have played a pivotal role in turning vision into reality, demonstrating that even the most visionary leaders rely on others to achieve their goals. Winston Churchill's wartime collaborations during World War II are a powerful testament to the transformative impact of relationships.

When Churchill became Prime Minister of Britain in 1940, the nation faced one of its darkest hours. Nazi Germany had overrun much of Europe, and the British Isles were under constant threat of invasion. Churchill understood that Britain could not win the war alone. To counter the Axis powers, he needed to forge alliances, most critically with the United States and the Soviet Union.

Building these relationships was no simple task. The United States, under President Franklin

D. Roosevelt, was initially reluctant to enter the war, adhering to a policy of isolationism. Meanwhile, the Soviet Union, led by Joseph Stalin, was an ideologically opposed regime with its own ambitions and suspicions. Churchill's challenge was to bridge these divides, creating a united front against a common enemy.

Churchill's ability to foster these alliances stemmed from his exceptional interpersonal skills. He was a master communicator, using his eloquence and wit to inspire confidence and convey urgency. His speeches, letters, and personal meetings with Roosevelt and Stalin were not merely exchanges of information— they were acts of persuasion and trust-building. Churchill appealed to shared values, such as the defense of freedom and the fight against tyranny, while also addressing the specific concerns of his allies.

For Roosevelt, Churchill emphasized the moral imperative of supporting Britain and the strategic importance of defeating Germany before the Axis powers became too strong. His ability to frame Britain's struggle as part of a larger narrative resonated with Roosevelt, ultimately leading to the passage of the Lend-Lease Act, which provided critical supplies and support to Britain.

With Stalin, Churchill adopted a pragmatic approach. Despite their ideological differences, he recognized the necessity of cooperation and worked to build a functional relationship based on mutual respect. The Tehran Conference in 1943, where Churchill, Roosevelt, and Stalin met in person, was a turning point in the war effort, laying the groundwork for coordinated military strategies that would ultimately lead to victory.

Churchill's alliances illustrate a profound truth about leadership: the ability to navigate and nurture relationships is as important as strategy or vision. Relationships provide access to resources, perspectives, and support that no leader can achieve alone. They also create a sense of shared purpose, transforming individual efforts into collective action.

Beyond the political realm, the importance of relationships is evident in the world of business and innovation. Consider the partnership between Bill Gates and Paul Allen, the co-found-

ers of Microsoft. Their complementary skills—
Gates' strategic thinking and Allen's technical
expertise—were instrumental in shaping Microsoft into one of the most influential technology
companies in history.

Their partnership thrived not because they
agreed on everything, but because they respected and valued each other's contributions. This
dynamic underscores the importance of trust
and mutual appreciation in any relationship.
By recognizing and leveraging each other's
strengths, Gates and Allen were able to navigate
challenges and capitalize on opportunities that
would have been insurmountable individually.

Philosophically, the significance of relationships
aligns with the teachings of Aristotle, who wrote
extensively about the value of friendship in his
Nicomachean Ethics. Aristotle viewed friendship
as a cornerstone of a virtuous and fulfilling life,
emphasizing that true friendships are based on
mutual respect and shared values. This perspective reminds us that relationships are not merely
transactional but deeply human, rooted in trust,
empathy, and collaboration.

For contemporary leaders, cultivating meaning-ful relationships involves more than networking or transactional exchanges. It requires a genuine commitment to understanding and supporting others. This begins with active listening—pay-ing attention to the concerns, aspirations, and perspectives of those around you. By showing empathy and curiosity, leaders can build trust and create an environment where collaboration flourishes.

It also involves a willingness to invest in rela-tionships over time. Churchill's alliances with Roosevelt and Stalin were not built overnight; they required patience, persistence, and adapt-ability. Similarly, business partnerships, men-torships, and team dynamics thrive when nur-tured through consistent communication and mutual respect.

Practical applications of this principle can be seen in organizational leadership. Teams that prioritize relationships often outperform those that focus solely on individual achievements. By fostering a culture of collaboration and support, leaders can unlock the collective potential of their teams, achieving outcomes that far surpass what any one person could accomplish alone.

On a personal level, the importance of relationships extends to mentorship and community.
Surrounding yourself with individuals who
challenge and inspire you can accelerate your
growth and broaden your horizons. Seek out
mentors who offer guidance and perspective,
as well as peers who share your values and
ambitions. These relationships not only enhance
your capabilities but also provide a sense of
belonging and purpose.

Ultimately, the power of relationships lies in
their ability to amplify impact. Churchill's wartime alliances, Gates and Allen's partnership,
and countless other examples remind us that
leadership is not about going it alone—it is
about building a network of allies who share
your vision and contribute to its realization.

For those who aspire to lead with impact, the
lesson is clear: relationships are not a luxury—
they are a necessity. By investing in connections
based on trust, empathy, and shared purpose,
leaders can navigate challenges, seize opportunities, and create lasting change. The journey of

leadership is not a solo endeavor—it is a collective one, enriched by the relationships we build and the allies we find along the way.

Influence and Persuasion

Leadership is not merely about authority; it is about influence—the ability to inspire, motivate, and guide others toward a common goal. Influence, when combined with the art of persuasion, transforms ideas into action. The most effective leaders are those who understand that persuasion is not about coercion but about connection. They use rhetorical skills, emotional intelligence, and authenticity to gain support and build consensus. History provides countless examples of leaders who mastered these techniques, creating movements and alliances that changed the course of history.

One of the most powerful demonstrations of influence and persuasion can be found in the leadership of Martin Luther King Jr. during the American Civil Rights Movement. King's ability to mobilize millions of people in the fight for racial equality was rooted in his profound understanding of rhetoric and human emotion. His speeches, including the iconic "I Have a Dream" address, were not just powerful because of their content but because of the way they connected with the hearts and minds of his audience.

King's rhetorical brilliance lay in his ability to weave together universal principles of justice with vivid imagery and personal narratives. He appealed to the shared values of his audience — freedom, equality, and the American dream — while also painting a vision of a better future. His words were not just aspirational; they were actionable, instilling a sense of urgency and purpose.

Beyond rhetoric, King's emotional intelligence was a cornerstone of his influence. He understood the fears and frustrations of his followers, as well as the resistance of his opponents. By addressing these emotions with empathy and authenticity, he was able to build trust and credibility. Even in the face of violence and hostility, King's unwavering commitment to nonviolence and reconciliation inspired admiration and respect, even among those who initially opposed him.

The techniques that King used—rhetorical skill and emotional intelligence—are not confined to history. They remain vital tools for leaders in all fields. The ability to communicate effectively and connect emotionally with others is what turns ideas into movements and strategies into results.

Another striking example of influence and persuasion comes from the business world, with the leadership of Steve Jobs. Jobs was not just a visionary innovator; he was a masterful storyteller who could inspire employees, investors, and consumers alike. His product launches were legendary, often described as performances rather than presentations.

Jobs understood that persuasion was about more than presenting facts—it was about creating a narrative that resonated with people's aspirations and emotions. When he introduced the iPhone in 2007, he didn't just describe its features; he framed it as a revolutionary device that would change the way people lived. His ability to make audiences believe in his vision was a key factor in Apple's success.

What set Jobs apart was his authenticity. He genuinely believed in the products he promoted, and that passion was contagious. People were drawn to his conviction and clarity of purpose, which made his influence all the more powerful.

The lessons from King and Jobs highlight that influence and persuasion are deeply human skills. They require leaders to connect with others on an emotional level, using authenticity and empathy to build relationships. This is where emotional intelligence becomes particularly important. Leaders with high emotional intelligence are adept at reading social cues, managing their own emotions, and responding to the needs of others.

Philosophically, the principles of influence and persuasion align with the teachings of Aristotle, who identified three key components of persuasion in his work *Rhetoric*: ethos, pathos, and logos. Ethos refers to the credibility of the speaker, pathos to the emotional appeal, and logos to the logical argument. Effective leaders balance these elements, establishing trust (ethos), connecting emotionally (pathos), and presenting compelling evidence (logos).

For contemporary leaders, mastering influence and persuasion begins with self-awareness. Understanding your own strengths, values, and communication style allows you to project authenticity and confidence. People are more likely to follow leaders who are genuine and consistent in their actions and words.

It also involves active listening. Persuasion is not about talking at people but engaging with them. By listening to the concerns and aspirations of your audience, you can tailor your message to address their needs and motivations. This creates a sense of alignment and shared purpose, making your message more compelling.

Practical applications of these principles can be seen in organizational leadership. For example, when introducing a new initiative, a leader who frames the change as an opportunity for growth and addresses employees' concerns with empathy is more likely to gain buy-in. Similarly, in sales and marketing, connecting with customers on an emotional level can make a product or service more appealing.

On a personal level, influence and persuasion are valuable skills in building relationships and achieving goals. Whether negotiating a promotion, resolving a conflict, or advocating for a cause, the ability to communicate effectively and connect emotionally can make all the difference.

Ultimately, the power of influence and persuasion lies in their ability to bring people together. Martin Luther King Jr., Steve Jobs, and countless other leaders demonstrate that persuasion is not about manipulation—it is about inspiring trust, fostering connection, and creating a shared vision. For those who aspire to lead with impact, the lesson is clear: to influence others, you must first connect with them. By mastering the art of communication and cultivating emotional intelligence, leaders can turn ideas into action and build a network of allies who share their vision for the future.

Creating Synergistic Teams

The power of collaboration lies in its ability to amplify individual strengths, creating a whole that is greater than the sum of its parts. Syner-

gistic teams—groups where members comple-
ment each other's skills and perspectives—are
the driving force behind some of history's most
remarkable achievements. Building such teams
requires more than assembling talented individuals; it demands a leader's ability to foster trust,
align goals, and cultivate an environment where
differences become assets rather than obstacles.
The story of the Wright brothers exemplifies the
transformative potential of synergistic teamwork.

Wilbur and Orville Wright were not the first to
dream of human flight, nor were they the most
resourced or formally educated. What set them
apart was their ability to work together as a
cohesive unit, leveraging their complementary
skills and shared vision. Wilbur, often described
as the more analytical and strategic of the two,
excelled at understanding the theoretical aspects of aerodynamics and problem-solving
complex challenges. Orville, on the other hand,
brought a hands-on, mechanical ingenuity to
their partnership, turning ideas into tangible
prototypes.

Their collaboration thrived on mutual respect

and a clear division of labor. The brothers trusted each other's expertise and were willing to challenge each other's assumptions in a constructive manner. This dynamic allowed them to iterate rapidly, combining Wilbur's meticulous calculations with Orville's practical experimentation to refine their designs.

The Wright brothers' ability to synthesize their strengths culminated in their historic flight at Kitty Hawk in 1903. It was not a single breakthrough that led to their success but a series of incremental improvements born out of their collaborative process. Their story underscores a key principle of synergistic teamwork: diversity of thought and skill is not a weakness—it is a strength that drives innovation.

The importance of complementary skill sets extends beyond aviation. In the realm of business, the partnership between Steve Jobs and Steve Wozniak at Apple illustrates how synergistic teams can revolutionize industries. Jobs, the visionary and marketer, brought a keen sense of design and an ability to captivate audiences with his ideas. Wozniak, the engineer, provided the technical expertise needed to turn those ideas into groundbreaking products.

Their collaboration produced the Apple I and Apple II computers, which laid the foundation for the personal computing revolution. While Jobs and Wozniak had different temperaments and approaches, their partnership worked because they shared a common goal and respected each other's contributions. By focusing on their respective strengths, they created a synergy that neither could have achieved alone.

For leaders, the challenge of creating synergistic teams begins with understanding the unique abilities and perspectives of each team member. This requires active listening and a genuine interest in what individuals bring to the table. Leaders must also create an environment where differences are valued and leveraged rather than suppressed.

A key aspect of fostering synergy is aligning team members around a shared vision. The Wright brothers were united by their dream of achieving flight, just as Jobs and Wozniak were driven by their desire to make computing accessible to the masses. A clear and compelling goal provides a sense of purpose that motivates individuals to work collaboratively, transcending personal egos and conflicts.

Philosophically, the concept of synergy aligns with the teachings of Taoism, particularly the principle of harmony through balance. In the *Tao Te Ching*, Lao Tzu writes, "When two great forces oppose each other, the victory will go to the one that knows how to yield." This perspective emphasizes the importance of flexibility and adaptability in achieving harmony, both within teams and in the broader context of leadership.

On a practical level, creating synergistic teams involves thoughtful composition and deliberate facilitation. Leaders must consider not only the technical skills of team members but also their interpersonal dynamics. Diversity in backgrounds, perspectives, and experiences can lead to richer problem-solving and more innovative solutions.

However, diversity alone is not enough; it must be accompanied by a culture of trust and psychological safety. Team members need to feel comfortable expressing their ideas and challenging each other without fear of judgment or retribution. This requires leaders to model vulnerability, encourage open communication, and address conflicts constructively.

Another critical element of synergy is recognizing and celebrating contributions. When individuals feel that their efforts are valued and acknowledged, they are more likely to engage fully and collaborate effectively. Leaders can foster this sense of recognition through regular feedback, public praise, and opportunities for professional growth.

The benefits of synergistic teams extend far beyond individual projects. They create a foundation for long-term success, fostering relationships and networks that can be leveraged in future endeavors. For example, the Wright brothers' collaborative spirit influenced the broader aviation industry, inspiring a culture of innovation and partnership that continues to this day.

In contemporary settings, organizations that prioritize teamwork and collaboration consistently outperform those that do not. Companies like Google and Pixar have built cultures that encourage cross-disciplinary collaboration, resulting in groundbreaking products and creative breakthroughs. By creating environments where teams can thrive, these organizations demonstrate the lasting impact of synergy.

On a personal level, the principles of synergistic teamwork can be applied to any collaborative effort, from professional projects to community initiatives. Start by identifying the strengths and perspectives of those you work with, and look for ways to align your efforts around a shared goal. Approach differences with curiosity and respect, recognizing that diversity is a source of strength.

Ultimately, creating synergistic teams is about embracing the collective potential of individuals. The stories of the Wright brothers, Jobs and Wozniak, and countless others remind us that no great achievement is accomplished in isolation. By fostering collaboration, leveraging complementary skills, and aligning efforts around a common purpose, leaders can unlock the full power of their teams, achieving results that are truly greater than the sum of their parts.

Leveraging Collective Power

The true strength of leadership lies not in individual effort but in the ability to harness the collective power of a group. When collaboration is executed effectively, it amplifies impact, enabling teams, organizations, and nations to achieve goals far beyond the reach of any single person. This principle was demonstrated on an unparalleled scale during Franklin D. Roosevelt's presidency, particularly through his coalition-building during World War II.

When the United States entered the war in 1941, Roosevelt faced a monumental challenge: leading a nation deeply divided in its perspectives on international involvement while uniting allies with diverse interests to defeat a common enemy. The stakes were enormous, and success depended on Roosevelt's ability to galvanize collective power across political, military, and cultural lines.

Roosevelt's coalition-building began at home, where he rallied Americans behind the war effort. The attack on Pearl Harbor had ignited a surge of patriotism, but sustaining support required more than emotion—it needed organization and purpose. Roosevelt established programs like the War Production Board, which coordinated industries to produce everything from airplanes to ammunition, transforming the U.S. into the "Arsenal of Democracy."

The mobilization of industry was not just a logistical feat; it was a testament to Roosevelt's ability to inspire collaboration among stakeholders with competing interests. Business leaders, labor unions, and government officials often clashed, but Roosevelt's steady leadership and willingness to mediate disputes ensured that the nation's resources were directed toward a common cause. By leveraging the collective power of these groups, Roosevelt created a production engine that would prove decisive in the Allied victory.

On the global stage, Roosevelt's coalition-building reached new heights with the formation of the Allied powers. This alliance, comprising nations with vastly different political systems and priorities, required delicate negotiation and mutual compromise. Roosevelt, along with

Winston Churchill and Joseph Stalin, forged a partnership that united capitalist democracies and communist regimes against the Axis powers.

The Tehran Conference of 1943 exemplified the complexities of this coalition. Roosevelt had to navigate tensions between Churchill's cautious approach and Stalin's demands for a second front in Europe. By fostering open communication and emphasizing shared goals, he ensured that the Allies remained unified despite their differences. This unity was critical in coordinating major campaigns, such as the D-Day invasion, which marked the beginning of the end for Nazi Germany.

Roosevelt's success in leveraging collective power lay in his ability to balance pragmatism with vision. He understood that collaboration required not only a shared purpose but also a recognition of individual contributions. By acknowledging the unique strengths of each ally—Britain's naval power, the Soviet Union's vast manpower, and America's industrial capacity—Roosevelt built a coalition that was greater than the sum of its parts.

This principle is not limited to wartime alliances; it applies to any context where collaboration is essential. In business, the power of collective effort is evident in the rise of open-source platforms like Linux. Developed through the contributions of programmers around the world, Linux has become one of the most widely used operating systems, powering everything from smartphones to supercomputers. The success of Linux demonstrates that collaboration, when effectively organized, can rival or surpass traditional hierarchical models.

The philosophy behind leveraging collective power aligns with the teachings of Confucius, who emphasized the importance of harmony and mutual respect in achieving societal goals. In the *Analects*, Confucius writes, "When the wind blows, the grass bends." This metaphor suggests that leadership is not about forcing compliance but about guiding and aligning others toward a common purpose.

For leaders, leveraging collective power begins with creating a clear and compelling vision. People are more likely to collaborate when they see how their efforts contribute to a larger goal. Roosevelt's framing of the war as a fight for freedom and democracy resonated with both citizens and allies, providing a unifying narrative that transcended individual interests.

Equally important is the ability to foster trust and accountability within the group. Collaboration thrives in environments where individuals feel valued and empowered to contribute. This requires leaders to listen actively, delegate effectively, and address conflicts constructively. Roosevelt's ability to mediate disputes among labor unions, business leaders, and foreign allies was a key factor in maintaining cohesion.

Another critical aspect of leveraging collective power is adaptability. Collaboration often involves navigating uncertainty and adjusting strategies based on evolving circumstances. During the war, Roosevelt demonstrated this adaptability by responding to shifting dynamics on the battlefield and within the alliance. His willingness to embrace new ideas and perspectives ensured that the coalition remained effective, even in the face of setbacks.

In contemporary settings, the principles of collective power can be applied to organizations, communities, and even personal endeavors. For example, leaders in the workplace can foster collaboration by building cross-functional teams that draw on diverse skills and perspectives. By creating a culture of inclusion and innovation, these leaders unlock the potential of their teams, driving creativity and productivity.

On a personal level, leveraging collective power involves recognizing the value of relationships and seeking out opportunities for collaboration. Whether working on a community project or pursuing a professional goal, surrounding yourself with supportive and talented individuals can amplify your efforts and expand your impact.

Ultimately, the power of collaboration lies in its ability to transcend individual limitations. Roosevelt's coalition, the open-source movement, and countless other examples remind us that great achievements are rarely the result of solitary effort. They are the product of collective determination, shaped by leaders who understand how to align and amplify the strengths of those around them.

For those who aspire to lead with impact, the lesson is clear: collaboration is not just a strategy—it is a necessity. By leveraging collective power, leaders can overcome challenges, seize opportunities, and create lasting change that benefits not only themselves but also the communities and organizations they serve.

CHAPTER 6: ADAPTING TO CHANGE – INNOVATING IN THE FACE OF UNCERTAINTY

Recognizing the Need for Change

In the ever-evolving landscape of leadership and innovation, one constant remains: change is inevitable. Those who succeed are often not the most talented or resourced but the most adaptable. Recognizing the need for change—sometimes before the full scope of necessity becomes apparent—is a skill that has propelled leaders throughout history to unparalleled achievements. Among these visionaries, Thomas Edison stands as a quintessential example of adapting to change, not merely as a response but as a proactive strategy for growth.

Edison's career began with an unrelenting focus on invention. From the phonograph to the motion picture camera, his workshop in Menlo Park, New Jersey, was a hive of creativity, earning him the moniker "The Wizard of Menlo Park." However, Edison soon realized that the act of invention alone was not enough to secure long-term success. The true impact of his work would only be realized through commercialization—transforming ideas into products that could reach the masses.

This shift in focus was most evident in Edison's work on the electric light bulb. By the late 1870s, electric lighting was a tantalizing concept, but existing designs were impractical for widespread use. Edison's genius lay not just in improving the bulb itself but in recognizing the need for an entire electrical system to support it. He envisioned a network of power generation and distribution that would make electric lighting accessible to homes and businesses.

This recognition required Edison to pivot from the role of inventor to that of entrepreneur and systems thinker. He established the Edison Electric Light Company and worked tirelessly to develop not only the light bulb but also generators, wiring, and even the first power station on Pearl Street in New York City. Edison's shift from isolated inventions to integrated systems marked a turning point in both his career and the broader history of technology.

The story of Edison's transition highlights a fundamental truth: recognizing the need for change often involves stepping back to see the bigger picture. For Edison, this meant understanding that his light bulb would remain a curiosity unless supported by a comprehensive infrastructure. This insight allowed him to anticipate market needs and position himself as a pioneer not just of electric lighting but of modern electricity itself.

The ability to recognize the need for change is equally vital in other contexts. During World War II, leaders across industries and governments were forced to adapt to unprecedented challenges. One striking example comes from the automotive industry, where manufacturers like Ford and General Motors shifted from producing cars to building military vehicles and aircraft.

This transformation, known as the "Arsenal of Democracy," was driven by necessity but executed with remarkable foresight. Leaders in these companies recognized that the skills and infrastructure they had developed for automobile production could be repurposed to meet the demands of war. This shift required not only technical innovation but also a cultural change, as companies reoriented their priorities to align with national objectives.

The success of this transition underscores the importance of agility in leadership. Recognizing the need for change is not simply about identifying problems; it is about envisioning solutions and rallying resources to implement them. Leaders who anticipate and embrace change position themselves to navigate uncertainty with confidence and purpose.

Philosophically, the concept of recognizing the need for change aligns with the teachings of Heraclitus, the ancient Greek philosopher who famously declared, "Change is the only constant in life." Heraclitus believed that understanding the inevitability of change was essential to living in harmony with the world. This perspective reminds us that resistance to change is futile; what matters is how we respond to it.

For contemporary leaders, recognizing the need for change begins with cultivating awareness. This involves paying attention to emerging trends, listening to feedback, and remaining open to new ideas. It also requires humility — the willingness to acknowledge when current strategies are no longer effective and to pivot accordingly.

Jeff Bezos, the founder of Amazon, offers a modern example of this principle in action. In the early days of Amazon, the company was primarily an online bookstore. However, Bezos recognized that the internet was reshaping consumer behavior and that Amazon's infrastructure could support a much broader range of products. This insight led to the expansion of Amazon into the "everything store," a transformation that revolutionized retail.

Bezos's ability to recognize the need for change did not stop there. He continually pushed Amazon to innovate, from the introduction of Amazon Prime to the development of cloud computing through Amazon Web Services (AWS). Each of these pivots was driven by a clear understanding of market dynamics and a willingness to adapt.

The practical applications of recognizing the need for change are as relevant for individuals as they are for organizations. On a personal level, this skill involves staying attuned to shifts in one's environment, whether in the workplace, relationships, or broader life circumstances. It requires self-reflection and a proactive mindset, asking questions like: What is no longer serving me? Where are new opportunities emerging?

In organizational contexts, leaders can foster a culture of adaptability by encouraging experimentation and rewarding initiative. This involves creating space for employees to explore new ideas and challenge existing norms. By normalizing change as a part of growth, leaders empower their teams to respond to uncertainty with creativity and resilience.

Ultimately, recognizing the need for change is about staying ahead of the curve. Thomas Edison, the wartime industrialists, and modern leaders like Jeff Bezos all demonstrate that change is not something to be feared—it is something to be embraced. By seeing change as an opportunity rather than a threat, leaders can navigate uncertainty, drive innovation, and achieve lasting success.

For those who aspire to lead with impact, the lesson is clear: change is inevitable, but progress is not. Recognizing the need for change is the first step in transforming challenges into opportunities, ensuring that you remain not just relevant but revolutionary in an ever-changing world.

Agility in Leadership

In times of uncertainty, agility becomes the hallmark of great leadership. It is not the strongest or the most prepared leaders who thrive, but those who can adapt quickly to shifting circumstances while maintaining focus on their goals. Agility in leadership is the ability to pivot, innovate, and make decisions with confidence in unpredictable environments. Throughout history, leaders who demonstrated agility in the face of chaos not only survived but excelled, leaving behind legacies of resilience and innovation. The lessons from wartime innovation offer some of the most compelling examples of this principle in action.

During World War II, the Allied forces faced unprecedented challenges that required rapid adjustments in strategy and resources. One striking example of agility in leadership can be seen in the development of radar technology by the British. At the outbreak of the war, Britain was vulnerable to aerial attacks by Germany's Luftwaffe. Conventional defense methods were inadequate to counter the speed and scale of this new form of warfare. Recognizing the threat, British scientists and military leaders worked tirelessly to develop radar systems capable of detecting enemy aircraft before they reached their targets.

The innovation of radar was not a solitary effort but a collaborative process that involved scientists, engineers, and military personnel working in unison. Leaders like Sir Robert Watson-Watt, often referred to as the "father of radar," exemplified agility by coordinating these diverse efforts and overcoming significant technical and logistical hurdles. Within months, Britain had established a network of radar stations known as the Chain Home system, which provided early warnings of incoming attacks and gave the Royal Air Force a critical advantage during the Battle of Britain.

This ability to pivot and innovate under pressure underscores a key aspect of agility in leadership: the willingness to embrace new ideas and adapt to unforeseen challenges. Radar technology was in its infancy at the time, and its development required leaders to take calculated risks, allocate resources to unproven solutions, and maintain a sense of urgency without succumbing to panic.

A similar demonstration of agility occurred in the United States with the Manhattan Project, the secret wartime effort to develop the atomic bomb. Faced with the possibility that Nazi Germany might achieve nuclear capability first, American leaders acted swiftly to assemble a team of the world's best scientists and engineers. Under the direction of General Leslie Groves and physicist J. Robert Oppenheimer, the Manhattan Project epitomized agile leadership.

The project demanded constant adaptation. Scientific breakthroughs had to be translated into practical engineering solutions, and logistical challenges—such as securing rare materials and constructing specialized facilities—required innovative thinking. Despite the immense pressure and moral complexities of their work, the leaders of the Manhattan Project maintained focus, enabling the development of a weapon that ultimately ended the war in the Pacific.

These historical examples illustrate that agility in leadership is not just about reacting to change; it is about anticipating it, preparing for it, and responding with clarity and purpose. Agility involves a balance between flexibility and decisiveness, allowing leaders to navigate uncertainty without losing sight of their objectives.

Philosophically, the concept of agility aligns with Sun Tzu's teachings in *The Art of War*. Sun Tzu emphasized the importance of adaptability in strategy, writing, "Be extremely subtle, even to the point of formlessness. Be extremely mysterious, even to the point of soundlessness. Thereby you can be the director of the opponent's fate." This perspective reminds us that agility is not just a reactive skill—it is a proactive mindset that enables leaders to shape their environments rather than be constrained by them.

In the modern era, agility in leadership is as relevant as ever. Consider the response of global businesses to the COVID-19 pandemic. Companies that demonstrated agility—whether by pivoting to remote work, reconfiguring supply chains, or introducing new digital offerings—were better positioned to weather the crisis. For example, Airbnb faced a dramatic decline in bookings at the start of the pandemic but quickly adapted by introducing online experiences, allowing hosts to offer virtual tours, classes, and workshops. This pivot not only sustained the platform's relevance but also created new revenue streams that continue to thrive.

For leaders, cultivating agility begins with embracing uncertainty as an opportunity for growth. This involves fostering a culture of experimentation and encouraging teams to take calculated risks. Leaders must be willing to challenge conventional wisdom, explore alternative solutions, and learn from failure.

Another critical aspect of agility is effective communication. In times of uncertainty, clear and consistent messaging helps build trust and maintain focus. Leaders who communicate their vision while remaining transparent about challenges inspire confidence and resilience within their teams.

Agility also requires a willingness to delegate

and empower others. During the Manhattan Project, for instance, General Groves relied on Oppenheimer's scientific expertise to guide the technical aspects of the project. By trusting his team and creating an environment where collaboration could flourish, Groves ensured that the project advanced efficiently despite its complexities.

On a personal level, agility in leadership involves cultivating a mindset of continuous learning. Stay informed about emerging trends, seek diverse perspectives, and remain open to feedback. By developing this mindset, individuals can respond to change with creativity and confidence, turning obstacles into opportunities.

Ultimately, agility in leadership is about navigating the unknown with grace and determination. Whether leading a nation through war, managing a company through a crisis, or pursuing personal goals in uncertain times, the ability to adapt is what sets successful leaders apart. The stories of wartime innovation and modern business pivots remind us that agility is not just a skill—it is a way of thinking that enables leaders to thrive in an unpredictable world.

For those who aspire to lead with impact, the lesson is clear: agility is not about having all the answers—it is about being ready to find them. By staying flexible, fostering collaboration, and maintaining focus, leaders can turn uncertainty into opportunity, driving progress even in the face of the unknown.

Reframing Challenges as Opportunities

In the realm of leadership, challenges are inevitable. Yet, the way leaders perceive and respond to these challenges often determines the difference between failure and success. Those who rise above adversity share a common trait: the ability to reframe challenges as opportunities. They see disruptions not as insurmountable obstacles but as catalysts for innovation and growth. Few leaders embody this mindset more vividly than Jeff Bezos, whose leadership at Amazon has transformed market disruptions into competitive advantages.

Bezos's journey as a leader began with a challenge that many would have found daunting:

launching an e-commerce platform at a time when the internet was in its infancy. In 1994, traditional retail dominated the market, and skeptics dismissed the idea of online shopping as impractical and risky. Rather than being deterred, Bezos recognized that this skepticism was an opportunity in disguise. He understood that the very newness of the internet presented a blank slate, allowing him to build something groundbreaking without the constraints of established norms.

Starting with books as his initial product category, Bezos laid the foundation for Amazon's customer-centric philosophy. However, the real test of his leadership came in the early 2000s, when the dot-com bubble burst. Many e-commerce startups failed during this period, and Amazon itself faced significant financial pressures. Its stock price plummeted, and critics questioned the company's long-term viability.

Instead of retreating, Bezos used the downturn as an opportunity to strengthen Amazon's position. He doubled down on his vision of making Amazon the "everything store," expanding into new product categories and investing heavily in technology and infrastructure. Recognizing that customer experience would be a key differentiator, he focused on innovations like one-click purchasing, personalized recommendations, and fast delivery.

One of Bezos's most significant pivots during this period was the creation of Amazon Web Services (AWS). Initially developed to support Amazon's own operations, AWS emerged as a solution to a broader challenge: the inefficiencies and costs associated with traditional IT infrastructure. By offering cloud computing services to other businesses, Amazon not only addressed its own challenges but also created a new revenue stream that would become one of its most profitable divisions.

Bezos's ability to reframe challenges as opportunities exemplifies a mindset that has driven some of history's most transformative innovations. This mindset involves looking beyond immediate setbacks to identify underlying opportunities. It requires curiosity, creativity, and a willingness to challenge conventional thinking.

The story of Walt Disney offers another powerful

example of this principle in action. In the 1920s, Disney's first animation studio, Laugh-O-Gram Films, went bankrupt due to financial difficulties and a lack of distribution partnerships. For many, such a failure might have marked the end of a career. Instead, Disney used this setback as a stepping stone, moving to Hollywood and founding a new studio with his brother Roy.

Disney's breakthrough came with the creation of Mickey Mouse, but even then, he faced significant challenges. Skeptics doubted the viability of synchronized sound in animation, and his team lacked the resources of larger studios. Yet, Disney reframed these challenges as opportunities to innovate. The result was *Steamboat Willie*, the first synchronized-sound cartoon, which catapulted Mickey Mouse to global fame and established Disney as a pioneer in the entertainment industry.

Reframing challenges as opportunities often involves embracing uncertainty and taking calculated risks. This principle is deeply rooted in philosophical traditions, particularly Stoicism. Marcus Aurelius, the Roman emperor and Stoic philosopher, wrote in his *Meditations*: "The impediment to action advances action. What stands in the way becomes the way." This perspective encourages leaders to view obstacles as essential components of progress, reminding us that adversity is not the enemy but the means to achieve greatness.

For contemporary leaders, applying this mindset begins with shifting how challenges are perceived. Instead of asking, "Why is this happening to me?" ask, "What can I learn from this?" This simple reframing turns setbacks into opportunities for growth and innovation.

Another key aspect of this approach is fostering a culture of experimentation. Jeff Bezos famously said, "Failure and invention are inseparable twins." At Amazon, this philosophy manifests in a willingness to test new ideas, even at the risk of failure. Initiatives like Prime Video, Alexa, and Amazon Go all originated from a willingness to explore uncharted territory, often in response to market disruptions.

Practical applications of this principle can be seen in industries as diverse as technology, healthcare, and education. During the COVID-

19 pandemic, for example, many companies faced the challenge of transitioning to remote work. Those that embraced the shift as an opportunity—investing in digital tools, rethinking workflows, and prioritizing employee well-being—emerged stronger and more adaptable.

On an individual level, reframing challenges as opportunities involves cultivating resilience and curiosity. It means approaching setbacks with a growth mindset, viewing failures as valuable learning experiences rather than definitive endings. By asking questions, seeking solutions, and remaining open to new possibilities, individuals can turn personal and professional challenges into catalysts for transformation.

Ultimately, the ability to reframe challenges as opportunities is what separates reactive leaders from proactive ones. Jeff Bezos, Walt Disney, and countless others demonstrate that disruptions, while daunting, are also fertile ground for creativity and growth. By embracing this mindset, leaders can not only navigate uncertainty but also shape it to their advantage, driving innovation and creating lasting impact.

For those who aspire to lead with vision and resilience, the lesson is clear: challenges are not roadblocks—they are opportunities in disguise. By changing how we see and respond to adversity, we unlock the potential to innovate, grow, and achieve greatness.

The Role of Resilience

Resilience is the quiet strength that underpins adaptability, enabling leaders to persevere through challenges, recover from setbacks, and emerge stronger on the other side. It is resilience that transforms uncertainty into a proving ground for innovation, shaping leaders who can endure not just the trials of the moment but the evolving demands of the future. The connection between adaptability and resilience is profound: while adaptability is the capacity to adjust to change, resilience is the fortitude to persist in the face of adversity. Together, they create the foundation for lasting success.

One of the most iconic examples of resilience in leadership is Winston Churchill's tenure as Prime Minister of Britain during World War II. When Churchill assumed office in 1940, the situation was dire. Much of Europe had fallen to Nazi Germany, and Britain stood alone as the last bastion of resistance in Western Europe. The Luftwaffe's relentless bombing campaign, known as the Blitz, devastated cities and tested the resolve of the British people.

Churchill's resilience became the backbone of Britain's survival and eventual triumph. He refused to entertain the idea of surrender, rallying his nation with speeches that combined honesty about the gravity of the situation with an unwavering determination to prevail. His famous declaration — "We shall fight on the beaches, we shall fight on the landing grounds, we shall fight in the fields and in the streets, we shall fight in the hills; we shall never surrender" — captured the spirit of resilience that defined his leadership.

Churchill's ability to maintain focus and inspire others in the darkest moments exemplifies the relationship between resilience and adaptability. Resilience provided the inner strength to endure the hardships of war, while adaptability allowed him to respond strategically to rapidly changing circumstances. Whether coordinating with the United States and the Soviet Union or adjusting military strategies in response to enemy actions, Churchill's leadership was a testament to the power of resilience in navigating uncertainty.

Modern examples of resilience often emerge in the context of business and technology. Consider the story of Howard Schultz and Starbucks. In the early 2000s, Starbucks faced a significant downturn. Overexpansion, economic pressures, and a loss of focus on customer experience led to declining sales and a tarnished brand image.

When Schultz returned as CEO in 2008, he demonstrated remarkable resilience in leading the company's turnaround. He made difficult decisions, including closing underperforming stores and halting expansions. More importantly, Schultz recommitted to the core values that had made Starbucks successful: quality, innovation, and customer connection. He introduced initiatives like the My Starbucks Rewards program, which deepened customer loyalty, and invested in employee training to improve service.

Schultz's leadership highlights the interplay between resilience and adaptability. His ability to stay true to Starbucks' mission while rethinking strategies and implementing bold changes enabled the company not only to recover but to thrive. By 2010, Starbucks had regained its footing, setting the stage for continued growth and innovation.

Resilience, however, is not merely about enduring challenges; it is about learning from them. The concept of resilience as a growth mechanism aligns with the philosophy of Friedrich Nietzsche, who famously said, "What does not kill me makes me stronger." This idea suggests that adversity is not just something to overcome but something to embrace as an opportunity for growth and self-discovery.

For leaders, cultivating resilience involves developing a mindset that views setbacks as temporary and solvable. It requires emotional regulation—the ability to remain calm and focused under pressure—and a sense of purpose that keeps long-term goals in sight even when short-term outcomes falter.

Another critical aspect of resilience is the ability to inspire it in others. Churchill's speeches, Schultz's commitment to Starbucks' mission, and countless other examples demonstrate that resilient leaders create resilient organizations. They foster cultures of trust, collaboration, and perseverance, empowering their teams to face challenges with confidence and creativity.

On a practical level, resilience can be cultivated through intentional habits and strategies. For individuals, building resilience involves maintaining physical and mental well-being, seeking support from mentors or peers, and reflecting on past successes to build confidence. For organizations, it involves creating systems that support adaptability, such as cross-functional teams, transparent communication, and opportunities for continuous learning.

One of the most inspiring lessons in resilience comes from the Apollo 13 mission. In 1970, a critical failure aboard the spacecraft jeopardized the lives of three astronauts. Faced with dwindling resources, limited time, and life-threatening conditions, NASA's team of engineers and scientists demonstrated extraordinary resilience.

Led by Flight Director Gene Kranz, the team worked tirelessly to devise solutions to problems as they arose, from improvising a carbon dioxide filtration system to recalculating the spacecraft's trajectory for reentry. Their motto—"Failure is not an option"—epitomized the resilience that drove their efforts. Against all odds, the mission ended with the safe return of the astronauts, a triumph of human ingenuity and perseverance.

The Apollo 13 story underscores that resilience is not about avoiding failure but about confronting it head-on with determination and creativity. It is a reminder that resilience and adaptability go hand in hand, enabling leaders to respond to challenges with clarity and resolve.

For contemporary leaders, the lessons of resilience are as relevant as ever. In a world marked by rapid change and uncertainty, the ability to adapt is essential, but it is resilience that provides the foundation for sustained success. Leaders who cultivate resilience in themselves and their teams are better equipped to navigate disruptions, seize opportunities, and achieve their vision.

Ultimately, resilience is not just a trait—it is a practice, a choice, and a commitment. It is the strength to endure, the courage to innovate, and the wisdom to grow. For those who aspire to lead with impact, resilience is not optional— it is indispensable. By embracing challenges, learning from setbacks, and fostering resilience in others, leaders can create lasting change and leave a legacy of strength and adaptability.

CHAPTER 7:
THE POWER OF
EXECUTION – TURNING
IDEAS INTO ACTION

Building Actionable Plans

Every great achievement begins with an idea, but the ability to translate vision into reality is what distinguishes leaders from dreamers. Execution—the art of turning ideas into action—is a defining trait of effective leadership. Central to this process is the creation of actionable plans: frameworks that break down ambitious goals into practical, achievable steps. The story of Henry Ford and his revolutionary assembly line serves as a powerful example of how actionable planning can transform industries and societies.

In the early 20th century, the automobile was a luxury item, accessible only to the wealthy. Henry Ford envisioned a future where cars were affordable and ubiquitous, revolutionizing transportation and reshaping modern life. However, realizing this vision required a radical shift in how cars were manufactured. Traditional methods were labor-intensive, inefficient, and costly, making mass production nearly impossible.

Ford's genius lay not just in his technical innovations but in his ability to reimagine the production process itself. He recognized that achieving his vision required a system that maximized efficiency while maintaining quality. Drawing inspiration from the meatpacking industry's conveyor systems and the principles of scientific management espoused by Frederick Winslow Taylor, Ford developed the moving assembly line.

The assembly line was a masterstroke of actionable planning. Ford broke down the complex process of car manufacturing into discrete, standardized tasks, assigning each worker a specific role. Parts were transported along a conveyor belt, allowing workers to focus on their individual tasks without moving from station to station. This approach minimized waste, reduced production time, and significantly lowered costs.

By 1913, Ford's assembly line was producing the Model T at unprecedented speeds. The time required to assemble a car dropped from over 12 hours to just 93 minutes, and the cost of the Model T plummeted, making it accessible to middle-class families. Ford's innovation not only revolutionized the automotive industry but also set the standard for modern manufacturing practices.

The success of Ford's assembly line highlights the power of breaking down grand visions into manageable steps. By identifying key processes, standardizing tasks, and implementing systematic improvements, Ford turned an ambitious goal into a tangible reality. This approach is a cornerstone of effective execution, applicable to any field or endeavor.

The principles behind actionable planning are deeply rooted in human psychology. The philosopher Aristotle emphasized the importance of habit and incremental progress, writing in his *Nicomachean Ethics*: "We are what we repeatedly do. Excellence, then, is not an act, but a habit." This perspective reminds us that achieving great things is often the result of small, consistent actions, each building on the last.

For leaders, creating actionable plans begins with clarity of purpose. A clear vision provides the foundation for effective execution, ensuring that every step aligns with the broader goal. This clarity must be accompanied by a detailed understanding of the resources, timelines, and constraints involved. Ford's success with the assembly line was not just about vision—it was about meticulous planning and a deep understanding of the production process.

Another critical element of actionable planning is prioritization. Not all tasks are equally important, and leaders must focus on the steps that will have the greatest impact. Ford's decision to standardize tasks and streamline workflows was a strategic choice that maximized efficiency without compromising quality. This principle applies equally to personal and organizational goals: by focusing on high-priority actions, leaders can drive progress more effectively.

In modern contexts, actionable planning is exemplified by companies like Tesla. Elon Musk's vision of accelerating the world's transition to sustainable energy is ambitious, but its execution relies on a series of carefully planned steps. From the development of the Tesla Roadster to the establishment of Gigafactories for battery production, each milestone has been part of a larger strategy to make electric vehicles mainstream.

Tesla's success also underscores the importance of flexibility in planning. While a clear roadmap is essential, leaders must remain adaptable, adjusting plans in response to changing circumstances. Ford faced numerous challenges during the implementation of the assembly line, from technical difficulties to labor disputes. By addressing these issues pragmatically and iterating on his designs, he ensured the success of his innovation.

For individuals, actionable planning involves translating personal or professional goals into specific, measurable steps. This might mean breaking a large project into smaller tasks, setting realistic deadlines, and tracking progress over time. By focusing on one step at a time, individuals can maintain momentum and avoid feeling overwhelmed.

Organizations, too, benefit from systematic planning. Effective leaders create structures that support execution, from clear communication channels to accountability mechanisms. By fostering a culture of collaboration and alignment, they ensure that every team member contributes meaningfully to the larger goal.

Ultimately, the ability to build actionable plans is what bridges the gap between aspiration and achievement. Henry Ford's assembly line, Elon Musk's strategic milestones, and countless other examples demonstrate that execution is not about luck—it is about discipline, focus, and perseverance.

For those who aspire to lead with impact, the lesson is clear: great ideas are only the beginning. By breaking down visions into actionable steps, prioritizing effectively, and remaining adaptable, leaders can turn their dreams into reality, leaving a legacy of progress and innovation.

Overcoming Execution Hurdles

Execution is where visions meet reality, and the path to turning ideas into action is rarely smooth. Leaders often encounter hurdles that test their resolve, creativity, and adaptability. These challenges range from resource constraints and operational inefficiencies to resistance from stakeholders and unforeseen external factors. The ability to navigate and overcome these obstacles is what sets successful leaders apart, ensuring that their goals remain achievable even in the face of adversity.

One of the most striking examples of overcoming execution hurdles comes from the Manhattan Project during World War II. The project's goal—to develop the world's first atomic bomb—was unprecedented in scope and urgency. It required the coordination of thousands of scientists, engineers, and military personnel across multiple sites, each working on different aspects of the project.

The challenges were immense. Resources like uranium and plutonium were scarce, and the scientific knowledge needed to create a nuclear chain reaction was still in its infancy. Additionally, the secrecy of the project posed logistical hurdles, as communication had to be tightly controlled to prevent leaks. Despite these obstacles, leaders like General Leslie Groves and physicist J. Robert Oppenheimer demonstrated remarkable ingenuity and perseverance.

One key strategy they employed was compartmentalization. By dividing the project into distinct tasks and assigning them to specialized teams, they minimized the risk of delays caused by information overload or miscommunication. This approach also allowed leaders to focus resources on the most critical aspects of the project, ensuring that progress continued even when setbacks occurred in specific areas.

Another pivotal moment in the Manhattan Project's execution was addressing the technical challenge of creating a reliable detonator for the bomb. Early prototypes were prone to failure, jeopardizing the entire endeavor. Instead of abandoning the concept, the team adopted an iterative approach, testing and refining designs until they achieved the desired result. This willingness to embrace trial and error highlights the importance of resilience and adaptability in overcoming execution hurdles.

Resource constraints are a common barrier to execution, and history provides numerous examples of leaders who turned scarcity into an advantage. During the Great Depression, Franklin D. Roosevelt's administration faced the dual challenge of widespread unemployment and a lack of funds for large-scale infrastructure projects.

Rather than letting these constraints derail his goals, Roosevelt launched the Works Progress Administration (WPA), a program that employed millions of Americans to build roads, bridges, schools, and other public works. By repurposing existing resources and mobilizing a willing workforce, the WPA not only addressed immediate economic needs but also laid the foundation for long-term national growth.

This ability to reframe constraints as opportunities is a hallmark of effective leadership. It requires a mindset that focuses on solutions rather than limitations, asking, "What can we do with what we have?" rather than "What can't we do?" This perspective aligns with the Stoic philosophy of accepting what is within our control and finding ways to act despite external challenges.

Resistance from stakeholders is another significant hurdle in execution. Whether it comes from employees, partners, or the public, resistance often stems from fear of change, lack of understanding, or misaligned incentives. Leaders

who address these concerns proactively can
turn resistance into support.

A compelling example of this is seen in the leadership of Nelson Mandela during South Africa's
transition from apartheid to democracy. Mandela faced enormous resistance from various
factions, including white minority groups who
feared retribution and black radicals who demanded immediate and sweeping reforms.

Mandela's approach was rooted in empathy and
dialogue. He engaged with opponents to understand their concerns and find common ground,
often making personal sacrifices to build trust.
His ability to navigate these tensions and rally
diverse groups behind a shared vision was instrumental in achieving a peaceful transition.

The lessons from Mandela's leadership highlight the importance of communication and
emotional intelligence in overcoming resistance.
Leaders who listen actively, address fears, and
align stakeholders with a compelling vision are
more likely to secure the support needed for
successful execution.

Practical applications of these principles are evident in modern business settings. Consider the launch of the iPhone in 2007. Steve Jobs and his team at Apple faced numerous hurdles, from technical challenges in developing the touchscreen interface to skepticism from telecom providers about the device's potential.

Jobs's response was to double down on Apple's strengths: design excellence, attention to detail, and relentless pursuit of innovation. By iterating on prototypes, conducting rigorous testing, and crafting a marketing narrative that emphasized the iPhone's revolutionary potential, Jobs overcame resistance and launched a product that redefined the industry.

For contemporary leaders, overcoming execution hurdles requires a combination of strategic planning, adaptability, and persistence. Start by identifying the most significant barriers to progress, whether they are resource-related, technical, or interpersonal. Break these barriers into smaller, more manageable challenges, and prioritize actions that address the root causes.

Equally important is fostering a culture of problem-solving within teams. Encourage collaboration, experimentation, and open communication, creating an environment where challenges are seen as opportunities for growth rather than insurmountable obstacles.

On a personal level, overcoming execution hurdles involves cultivating resilience and maintaining focus. Setbacks are inevitable, but leaders who stay committed to their goals and approach problems with curiosity and creativity are more likely to succeed.

Ultimately, the ability to overcome execution hurdles is what transforms ideas into reality. The Manhattan Project, the WPA, Mandela's reconciliation efforts, and countless other examples remind us that challenges are not roadblocks—they are stepping stones. By addressing obstacles with determination and ingenuity, leaders can navigate even the most complex paths, ensuring that their visions are not only realized but sustained.

The Discipline of Consistency

Execution is not a single act but a sustained

effort over time, and the most impactful leaders understand that consistency is the engine of progress. It is through steady, focused action that ideas evolve into achievements and visions transform into legacies. The discipline of consistency requires resilience, persistence, and an unwavering commitment to the goal, even in the face of distractions, setbacks, or monotony. Few leaders exemplify this principle as powerfully as Oprah Winfrey, whose career is a testament to the transformative power of sustained effort.

Oprah's journey to becoming one of the most influential figures in media and philanthropy was not marked by overnight success. Born into poverty in rural Mississippi, she faced numerous challenges in her early years, including discrimination, personal trauma, and financial instability. Yet, her ability to remain consistent in her pursuit of excellence allowed her to rise above these circumstances and carve out a path that redefined television and inspired millions.

When Oprah began hosting *The Oprah Winfrey Show* in 1986, the talk show format was already a crowded and competitive space. Many doubted her ability to stand out in a field dominated by established personalities. However, Oprah's vision for her show was clear: she wanted to create a platform that not only entertained but also educated, uplifted, and connected viewers on a deeper level.

This vision demanded unwavering consistency in execution. Oprah's dedication to authenticity and quality content became the cornerstone of her success. She meticulously prepared for each episode, ensuring that topics were relevant, discussions were meaningful, and guests were impactful. Over the course of 25 years, Oprah hosted more than 4,500 episodes, each a testament to her disciplined approach to her craft.

What set Oprah apart was her ability to maintain this level of focus and effort over decades. While other shows rose and fell, *The Oprah Winfrey Show* remained a cultural institution, influencing public discourse and shaping trends. This consistency was not just about maintaining high standards; it was about evolving with the times while staying true to her core values.

Oprah's career offers a profound lesson in the power of small, consistent actions. By showing up every day with the same level of commitment and passion, she built a platform that transcended entertainment and became a force for positive change. This principle aligns with Aristotle's observation that "excellence is not an act, but a habit." Consistency, in this sense, is the bridge between intention and accomplishment.

The discipline of consistency is not without its challenges. The allure of shortcuts, the weight of fatigue, and the pressure of external expectations can all threaten to derail even the most focused efforts. Oprah herself faced moments of doubt and adversity, from navigating controversial topics to managing the complexities of a growing media empire. However, her ability to stay grounded and aligned with her purpose enabled her to persevere.

Consistency is not just about repetition; it is about intentionality. Leaders who are consistent in their actions must also be consistent in their values, ensuring that every decision aligns with their vision and principles. This alignment fosters trust and credibility, both of which are essential for sustained success.

Another historical example of the power of consistency comes from the world of science. Marie Curie, the pioneering physicist and chemist, spent years conducting meticulous experiments that ultimately led to the discovery of radium and polonium. Her groundbreaking work required an extraordinary level of discipline, as she meticulously sifted through tons of pitchblende ore to isolate minute quantities of radioactive elements.

Curie's dedication to her research exemplifies the connection between consistency and perseverance. She faced numerous challenges, from financial constraints to societal prejudices against women in science. Yet, her unwavering focus and disciplined approach allowed her to achieve breakthroughs that revolutionized our understanding of radioactivity and earned her two Nobel Prizes.

For leaders, cultivating the discipline of consistency involves creating routines and habits that support long-term goals. This might mean setting aside dedicated time for strategic planning, regularly reviewing progress, or fostering a culture of accountability within teams. By establishing these structures, leaders ensure that consistent effort becomes second nature, even in the face of competing priorities.

Consistency also requires resilience—the ability to stay the course despite setbacks. Oprah's career, for example, was not without failures, but her willingness to learn from mistakes and adapt ensured that these moments became stepping stones rather than stumbling blocks.

On a personal level, the discipline of consistency can be cultivated through mindfulness and reflection. Taking the time to clarify one's values and priorities provides a foundation for intentional action. Setting realistic goals, tracking progress, and celebrating small victories help maintain motivation and momentum.

For organizations, consistency is a key driver of trust and loyalty. Companies that consistently deliver value to their customers, treat employees with respect, and uphold ethical standards build reputations that endure. This principle is evident in brands like Coca-Cola, which has maintained its identity and quality over more than a century, adapting to changing markets while remaining true to its core promise.

Ultimately, the discipline of consistency is about building momentum. Each small, deliberate action compounds over time, creating a ripple effect that leads to meaningful change. Whether it is Oprah Winfrey reshaping the media landscape, Marie Curie unlocking the secrets of the atom, or a leader guiding their team toward a shared goal, consistency is the thread that weaves intention into achievement.

For those who aspire to lead with impact, the lesson is clear: success is not a single moment but a series of moments, each defined by the effort and intention we bring to it. By committing to the discipline of consistency, leaders can turn ideas into enduring legacies, inspiring others to follow their example and build a future defined by purpose and perseverance.

Measuring and Refining Success

Execution is not a static process; it is dynamic, iterative, and constantly evolving. Successful leaders understand that implementing a plan is only the beginning. To ensure sustained progress and meaningful impact, they measure results, seek feedback, and make continuous adjustments. The power of feedback loops and data-driven refinement lies in their ability to transform good ideas into great achievements, ensuring that every step aligns with the ultimate vision.

One of the most profound examples of leveraging feedback loops to refine execution comes from the aerospace industry during the development of the Apollo program. In 1961, President John F. Kennedy set an ambitious goal for the United States: to land a man on the moon and return him safely to Earth before the end of the decade. This vision was as inspiring as it was daunting, requiring the combined efforts of NASA's best minds, advanced technology, and unwavering commitment.

However, the path to the moon was far from straightforward. Early missions like Apollo 1 faced significant setbacks, including a tragic fire that claimed the lives of three astronauts during a ground test. This failure could have derailed the program, but NASA's leaders treated it as an opportunity to learn and improve. They conducted a thorough investigation, identified design flaws, and implemented rigorous safety protocols to prevent future tragedies.

Throughout the Apollo program, feedback loops played a critical role in refining execution. Each mission built on the lessons of its predecessors, from the orbital tests of Apollo 7 to the lunar lander trials of Apollo 9. Data collected during these missions informed design adjustments, procedural changes, and risk mitigation strategies. By the time Apollo 11 launched in 1969, the program had evolved into a finely tuned operation, culminating in one of humanity's greatest achievements: landing on the moon.

The Apollo program's success underscores the importance of measuring progress and using feedback to guide refinement. Leaders who embrace this iterative approach are better equipped to navigate uncertainty, overcome challenges, and achieve their goals with precision and efficiency.

At its core, measuring and refining success is about maintaining alignment between actions and objectives. Without regular evaluation, even the most well-intentioned efforts can drift off course. This principle is evident in the business world, where leaders use performance metrics and customer feedback to ensure that their strategies deliver value.

Consider the example of Netflix. In its early years, the company faced stiff competition from traditional video rental stores like Blockbuster. Netflix's subscription model offered an innovative alternative, but its execution needed refinement to stay ahead of the curve.

One of Netflix's key strategies was its use of data to understand customer preferences and optimize its offerings. By analyzing viewing habits, Netflix identified trends and tailored its content library to meet audience demands. This data-driven approach also informed the company's transition to streaming, a bold pivot that anticipated the decline of physical rentals and revolutionized how people consume entertainment.

Netflix's ability to measure and refine its strategies has been a cornerstone of its success. Today, the company continues to leverage feedback loops, using algorithms and user data to personalize recommendations and develop original content that resonates with its audience.

This emphasis on continuous improvement aligns with the teachings of kaizen, a Japanese philosophy that emphasizes small, incremental changes for long-term success. Kaizen encourages leaders to view improvement as a journey rather than a destination, fostering a mindset of curiosity and adaptability.

For leaders, implementing feedback loops begins with identifying the right metrics. These metrics should provide meaningful insights into progress, highlighting areas of strength and opportunities for growth. For example, a company might track key performance indicators (KPIs) such as revenue growth, customer satisfaction, or employee engagement.

Equally important is creating a culture of feedback within teams and organizations. Leaders who encourage open communication and constructive criticism empower their teams to identify and address challenges proactively. This culture fosters trust, collaboration, and innovation, ensuring that every voice contributes to the refinement process.

On a personal level, measuring and refining success involves regular self-assessment. Reflecting on one's actions, seeking feedback from mentors or peers, and setting new goals based on lessons learned are all practices that support growth and improvement.

The role of resilience cannot be overstated in this process. Measuring success often reveals gaps or failures, which can be disheartening without the right mindset. Leaders who view setbacks as opportunities for learning are better equipped to adapt and refine their strategies. The Apollo program's response to tragedy, Netflix's evolution in the face of competition, and countless other examples demonstrate that resilience is the foundation of iterative progress.

Another essential aspect of refining execution is embracing technology and innovation. Tools like data analytics, project management software, and artificial intelligence provide leaders with real-time insights that inform decision-making. By leveraging these tools, leaders can identify trends, anticipate challenges, and implement changes with greater efficiency and accuracy.

Ultimately, the process of measuring and refining success is a testament to the power of adaptability and continuous learning. Leaders who prioritize feedback loops and data-driven adjustments ensure that their efforts remain aligned with their goals, even as circumstances evolve.

For those who aspire to lead with impact, the lesson is clear: execution is not a one-time effort but an ongoing commitment. By measuring progress, embracing feedback, and refining strategies, leaders can transform their ideas into enduring achievements, leaving a legacy of excellence and innovation.

CHAPTER 8: LEAVING A LEGACY – STRATEGIES THAT ENDURE BEYOND THEIR TIME

Defining an Enduring Legacy

True leadership transcends the boundaries of time. While many leaders excel within the moments they inhabit, those who leave a lasting impact think beyond their immediate circumstances. They craft legacies that endure, shaping future generations and inspiring progress long after their direct influence has waned. The essence of an enduring legacy lies not merely in achievements but in the systems, values, and examples left behind.

Few figures embody this principle more profoundly than Nelson Mandela, whose legacy of reconciliation and justice continues to resonate globally. Mandela's work during and after the dismantling of apartheid in South Africa was marked by an unwavering commitment to healing a fractured nation. His presidency, from 1994 to 1999, was not about accumulating power or personal accolades; it was about laying the foundation for a sustainable and unified democracy.

Mandela's legacy was meticulously crafted through intentional choices. One of his most

pivotal decisions was to advocate for reconciliation rather than retribution. After spending 27
years in prison, he emerged with a message of
forgiveness, recognizing that vengeance would
perpetuate the cycle of hatred and violence. His
establishment of the Truth and Reconciliation
Commission (TRC) was a groundbreaking step
in addressing the atrocities of apartheid.

The TRC provided a platform for victims to
share their stories and for perpetrators to seek
amnesty through honest confessions. This process, while imperfect, allowed South Africa to
confront its painful history and move forward
with a collective sense of accountability and
healing. Mandela's insistence on fostering dialogue and understanding, even in the face of
resistance, set a powerful example for future
leaders.

What makes Mandela's legacy enduring is its
universality. His principles of forgiveness, empathy, and justice are not confined to South
Africa—they are lessons that have inspired
movements for equality and reconciliation
worldwide. By embedding these values into
South Africa's political and social frameworks,

Mandela ensured that his vision would outlive him, influencing not only his country but the global community.

The concept of legacy extends beyond political leaders to visionaries in other fields. Consider the example of Jane Goodall, whose pioneering work with chimpanzees revolutionized the field of primatology and conservation. Goodall's legacy is not limited to her scientific discoveries; it encompasses her lifelong advocacy for environmental sustainability and animal welfare.

Goodall recognized early in her career that her work would have limited impact if it ended with her. To ensure the longevity of her vision, she established the Jane Goodall Institute, an organization dedicated to research, conservation, and education. By creating a network of committed individuals and empowering communities to take ownership of conservation efforts, Goodall built a legacy that continues to thrive.

Her emphasis on youth engagement through programs like Roots & Shoots demonstrates the importance of planting seeds for the future. By inspiring young people to care for the planet and its inhabitants, Goodall has ensured that her mission will be carried forward by the next generation. Her legacy reminds us that enduring impact often lies in the ability to inspire and empower others.

Philosophically, the idea of leaving a legacy aligns with the ancient Greek concept of *kleos*, often translated as "glory" or "renown." In Homeric epics like the *Iliad* and the *Odyssey*, heroes seek *kleos* through acts of valor that will be remembered long after their deaths. However, a modern interpretation of *kleos* shifts the focus from personal glory to collective benefit. True legacy is not about immortalizing oneself but about creating something of lasting value for others.

For contemporary leaders, defining an enduring legacy involves clarity of purpose and intentionality. It requires a long-term perspective, considering how today's actions will shape tomorrow's outcomes. Leaders who wish to leave a meaningful legacy must ask themselves: What principles do I want to embed in my work? How can I ensure that my vision remains relevant and impactful over time?

Practical applications of this mindset are evident in business, education, and social movements. Organizations that prioritize sustainability, for example, often design systems that balance short-term profitability with long-term environmental and social benefits. Patagonia, a leader in sustainable business practices, exemplifies this approach. By integrating environmental stewardship into its core operations and supporting grassroots activism, the company has created a legacy that extends beyond its products.

Another essential aspect of defining an enduring legacy is empowering others. Leaders like Mandela and Goodall understood that their visions could not be realized in isolation. By cultivating successors, building networks, and fostering a culture of shared responsibility, they ensured that their work would continue to flourish.

This principle is particularly relevant in mentorship. Leaders who invest in the growth and development of others create ripple effects that extend far beyond their direct influence. A mentor's guidance, encouragement, and wisdom can shape the trajectory of future leaders, amplifying their impact over time.

An enduring legacy also requires adaptability. As circumstances evolve, the systems and values a leader establishes must remain flexible enough to address new challenges. Walt Disney's creative empire is a prime example. Disney's commitment to storytelling and innovation has allowed his vision to endure for nearly a century, evolving with technological advancements and cultural shifts while staying true to its core mission of bringing joy to audiences.

Ultimately, defining an enduring legacy is about more than achieving success—it is about creating a foundation for others to build upon. It is about leaving behind something that grows, inspires, and transforms. Leaders who focus on legacy are not bound by the constraints of their own time; they think in terms of generations, crafting strategies that endure and adapt.

For those who aspire to lead with purpose, the lesson is clear: the true measure of leadership is not what you achieve during your lifetime but what you leave behind. By embedding values, creating systems of sustainability, and empowering others, leaders can ensure that their work resonates long after they are gone, shaping a future defined by progress, equity, and shared prosperity.

Creating Systems for Sustainability

Great leaders understand that their vision must extend beyond their lifetimes to achieve true impact. To ensure their work endures, they build systems that embed their principles into the fabric of organizations, movements, or communities. These systems serve as vehicles for sustainability, enabling ideas to evolve while remaining grounded in the values and goals of their creators. Walt Disney's creative empire is a shining example of how systems can sustain innovation, creativity, and cultural influence for decades.

Walt Disney's journey began with a simple yet profound vision: to create stories that brought joy and wonder to audiences of all ages. From humble beginnings as an animator, Disney expanded his aspirations to include full-length films, theme parks, and eventually a global entertainment empire. What set Disney apart was his ability to transform this vision into a self-sustaining system that continued to flourish long after his death in 1966.

At the heart of Disney's system was a culture of storytelling and innovation. He established the Walt Disney Studios as a creative power-house, fostering collaboration among writers, animators, and directors to produce timeless classics like *Snow White and the Seven Dwarfs* and *Fantasia*. Recognizing the importance of preserving the quality and magic of his brand, Disney implemented rigorous standards and processes that became ingrained in the studio's DNA.

This culture extended to Disneyland, which Disney envisioned not just as an amusement park but as a living storybook. The creation of Disneyland in 1955 was revolutionary, blending storytelling, technology, and immersive experiences in a way that had never been done before. To ensure the park's continued success, Disney established systems for maintaining quality, adapting to changing audience expectations, and fostering innovation.

One key element of Disney's sustainability strategy was his investment in talent and leadership development. He surrounded himself with individuals who shared his passion and could carry his vision forward. Figures like Roy Disney, his brother and business partner, and a cadre of creative leaders ensured that the company remained true to its mission while embracing new opportunities.

Today, The Walt Disney Company stands as a testament to the power of sustainability through systems. From animated classics to Marvel blockbusters, Disney's empire has evolved to reflect changing times while maintaining its core values of storytelling, imagination, and excellence.

The importance of creating systems for sustainability is not confined to entertainment. Leaders in other fields have used similar approaches to embed their principles and ensure the longevity of their work. In the world of social reform, Jane Addams, a pioneering social worker and founder of Hull House in Chicago, provides a compelling example.

Hull House, established in 1889, was more than a settlement house for impoverished immigrants; it was a comprehensive system for social change. Addams designed Hull House as a hub for education, healthcare, and advocacy, addressing the root causes of poverty and inequality. She collaborated with community members, policymakers, and philanthropists to create programs that empowered individuals and improved living conditions.

What made Hull House sustainable was its focus on systems thinking. Addams recognized that individual initiatives, while important, were insufficient to create lasting change. She worked to institutionalize her principles through education and policy reform, influencing legislation on labor rights, public health, and education. Hull House became a model for similar efforts across the United States, ensuring that Addams's vision continued to inspire social progress long after her time.

For contemporary leaders, creating systems for sustainability involves several key considerations. First, it requires a clear articulation of principles and values. These principles serve as the foundation for decision-making, guiding actions and ensuring alignment with the leader's vision.

Second, leaders must build structures that enable collaboration and innovation. This might include organizational frameworks, training programs, or technological platforms that facilitate growth and adaptability. For Walt Disney, this meant creating departments and teams that could independently drive creativity and operational excellence.

Third, sustainability demands investment in people. Empowering others to carry the vision forward is critical for long-term success. This involves not only identifying and nurturing talent but also fostering a culture of ownership and accountability. Leaders who inspire their teams to take initiative and innovate create a ripple effect that amplifies their impact.

Philosophically, the concept of sustainability aligns with the teachings of Confucianism, which emphasizes the importance of harmony, order, and continuity in society. Confucius taught that a well-ordered society depends on ethical leadership and the cultivation of virtuous behavior. Leaders who create systems that reflect these values contribute to the stability and prosperity of their communities.

On a practical level, sustainability is supported by tools like strategic planning, data-driven decision-making, and feedback loops. Organizations that use these tools to monitor progress, assess risks, and adapt to change are better equipped to thrive over time.

One modern example of sustainability in action is Patagonia, a company that has embedded environmental stewardship into its business model. By committing to sustainable sourcing, reducing waste, and supporting grassroots activism, Patagonia has created a system that aligns profitability with purpose. This approach not only benefits the environment but also reinforces the company's brand identity and customer loyalty.

Ultimately, creating systems for sustainability is about ensuring that a leader's vision remains relevant and impactful in a changing world. It requires foresight, adaptability, and a commitment to shared values. Leaders who build these systems leave behind more than accomplishments—they leave a legacy of progress, innovation, and possibility.

For those who aspire to lead with purpose, the lesson is clear: sustainability is not an afterthought; it is the cornerstone of enduring success. By embedding principles into the fabric of organizations, movements, or communities, leaders can ensure that their work continues to inspire and transform for generations to come.

Mentorship and Succession

No leader, no matter how brilliant or driven, can single-handedly ensure the longevity of their vision. The enduring impact of leadership depends on the ability to empower others to carry the torch, adapting the vision to meet future challenges while remaining true to its essence. Mentorship and succession are critical elements of this process, as they transform individual contributions into collective, intergenerational progress.

Mahatma Gandhi's life and work exemplify the

power of mentorship and succession in sustaining a movement. Gandhi's leadership in India's struggle for independence from British colonial rule was marked by his ability to inspire and mobilize millions through his principles of nonviolence (*ahimsa*) and civil disobedience. However, Gandhi understood that the success of the independence movement hinged not on his personal efforts alone but on the empowerment of others to lead, innovate, and take ownership of the cause.

Gandhi's approach to mentorship was rooted in his belief in self-reliance and collective responsibility. He cultivated relationships with individuals from diverse backgrounds, nurturing their potential and encouraging them to contribute to the movement in their unique ways. Leaders like Jawaharlal Nehru, who would go on to become India's first Prime Minister, and Vallabhbhai Patel, a key architect of India's integration as a unified nation, were profoundly influenced by Gandhi's teachings and guidance.

Through his mentorship, Gandhi instilled a deep commitment to the values of nonviolence and justice, ensuring that these principles would continue to guide India's political and social evolution. Even after his assassination in 1948, Gandhi's legacy endured through the leaders he inspired and the institutions he helped shape. His ability to pass on the torch was not just a testament to his leadership but a reflection of his understanding that lasting change requires collective effort.

The importance of mentorship and succession is not confined to political movements. In business, philanthropy, and the arts, leaders who invest in the growth and development of others amplify their impact and create pathways for sustained innovation.

Consider the example of Andrew Carnegie, the steel magnate and philanthropist whose wealth and influence shaped American industry and society in the late 19th and early 20th centuries. Carnegie was not only a visionary entrepreneur but also a mentor who believed in the transformative power of education and opportunity.

Carnegie's commitment to mentorship is perhaps best exemplified by his support for libraries and educational institutions. He funded the construction of over 2,500 libraries worldwide, providing countless individuals with access to knowledge and resources. His establishment of the Carnegie Corporation, a foundation dedicated to advancing education and scientific research, ensured that his vision for a more informed and empowered society would continue long after his death.

What made Carnegie's legacy enduring was his ability to institutionalize his principles through mentorship and philanthropy. By creating structures that enabled others to learn, innovate, and lead, he ensured that his contributions would have a ripple effect across generations.

Mentorship is not only about imparting knowledge or skills; it is about fostering a mindset of empowerment and adaptability. Effective mentors recognize the unique strengths and potential of each individual, guiding them to find their own paths while staying aligned with shared values. This approach creates a sense of ownership and accountability, enabling mentees to take initiative and drive progress independently.

Succession, on the other hand, involves the deliberate planning and preparation for leadership transitions. Leaders who neglect succession risk jeopardizing the continuity of their work, as the absence of a clear plan can lead to fragmentation, confusion, and loss of direction.

In the corporate world, companies like Apple have faced challenges in maintaining leadership continuity. When Steve Jobs, the visionary behind the company's resurgence, stepped down due to health issues, Apple's future seemed uncertain. However, Jobs's mentorship of Tim Cook, who succeeded him as CEO, provided a critical bridge. Cook's operational expertise and alignment with Jobs's values allowed Apple to maintain its innovative edge while adapting to new market realities.

Succession planning is particularly important in movements or organizations that rely on charismatic leadership. Without a clear strategy for passing the baton, such movements risk losing momentum or splintering after the departure of a central figure. Gandhi's emphasis on empowering local leaders and fostering grassroots participation mitigated this risk, ensuring that

India's independence movement remained resilient even in the face of his absence.

Philosophically, the importance of mentorship and succession aligns with the Confucian ideal of the *junzi*, or "noble person," who strives to cultivate virtue and elevate others. In Confucian thought, leadership is not about domination but about fostering harmony and collective progress. By guiding others to achieve their potential, leaders fulfill their duty to society and ensure the continuity of virtuous action.

For contemporary leaders, mentorship and succession require intentionality and humility. Effective mentors approach their role with a mindset of service, prioritizing the growth and well-being of those they guide. Succession planning, meanwhile, demands foresight and a willingness to let go of control, trusting others to carry the vision forward.

Practical strategies for mentorship include creating opportunities for learning and collaboration, providing constructive feedback, and modeling the values and behaviors that align with the vision. Succession planning involves identifying potential leaders, providing them with the tools and experiences they need to succeed, and fostering a culture of accountability and shared purpose.

Ultimately, mentorship and succession are acts of faith in the future. They reflect a leader's belief in the enduring value of their work and their commitment to empowering others to build on it. Gandhi's guidance of India's leaders, Carnegie's investment in education, and countless other examples remind us that the greatest leaders are those who inspire and enable others to lead.

For those who aspire to leave a lasting legacy, the lesson is clear: leadership is not a solo endeavor. By mentoring others and preparing for the future, leaders create a foundation for progress that transcends their individual contributions, ensuring that their vision continues to thrive and evolve for generations to come.

The Timelessness of Bold Strategies

The most powerful strategies transcend the eras in which they are conceived, leaving behind a legacy that continues to influence and inspire. These strategies endure because they are rooted in universal principles—ideas that address fundamental human needs, challenges, and aspirations. While bold strategies often emerge from specific circumstances, their adaptability ensures their relevance across time and contexts, shaping the future in ways their creators could never fully anticipate.

The story of Alexander the Great illustrates the timelessness of bold strategies. By the time of his death at just 32 years old, Alexander had forged one of the largest empires in history, stretching from Greece to India. His military conquests were extraordinary, but it was his strategic approach to governance and cultural integration that cemented his enduring legacy.

Alexander's bold strategy was rooted in his vision of a unified world. Unlike many conquerors who imposed their culture on subjugated peoples, Alexander sought to blend cultures, fostering mutual respect and collaboration. He encouraged intermarriage between Macedonians and Persians, adopted elements of local customs, and founded cities that became hubs of

cultural exchange. This approach not only sta-
bilized his vast empire but also laid the groundwork for the Hellenistic Age, a period marked
by remarkable advancements in art, science, and
philosophy.

Alexander's strategy remains relevant today
because it highlights the power of inclusivity
and collaboration. In a world that is increasingly interconnected, his vision of unity through
diversity offers valuable lessons for leaders navigating global challenges. By embracing bold
strategies that prioritize understanding and
integration, modern leaders can create solutions
that resonate across cultures and generations.

Another compelling example of timeless strategy comes from the civil rights movement in the
United States, led by figures like Martin Luther
King Jr. Dr. King's approach to achieving racial
equality was deeply influenced by the principles of nonviolence, which he adapted from
Mahatma Gandhi.

Dr. King's bold strategy was to confront injustice
not with violence or anger but with courage and
compassion. Through peaceful protests, boy-

cotts, and eloquent appeals to moral conscience, he galvanized a movement that transformed American society. The 1963 March on Washington for Jobs and Freedom, where Dr. King delivered his iconic "I Have a Dream" speech, exemplified the power of this approach.

The enduring impact of Dr. King's strategy lies in its moral clarity and universal appeal. Nonviolence is not just a tactic; it is a philosophy that transcends political and cultural boundaries, offering a path to justice that is both principled and pragmatic. Decades after Dr. King's assassination, his vision continues to inspire movements for equality and human rights around the world.

What makes these bold strategies timeless is their foundation in values that resonate with the human spirit: unity, justice, and progress. These values act as guiding stars, ensuring that strategies remain relevant even as circumstances evolve. Leaders who anchor their strategies in such principles create legacies that adapt and endure.

Philosophically, the timelessness of bold strategies can be understood through the lens of Aristotle's concept of *telos*, or purpose. Aristotle argued that every action aims toward an ultimate goal, and the most meaningful endeavors are those aligned with a higher purpose. Bold strategies that endure are those that align with universal goals—such as fostering understanding, advancing knowledge, or improving the human condition.

For leaders, crafting timeless strategies requires a balance of vision and adaptability. It involves looking beyond immediate challenges to consider the long-term impact of decisions. This perspective is evident in the work of Nelson Mandela, whose strategy for reconciliation in post-apartheid South Africa prioritized healing and unity over retribution. Mandela's focus on creating a just and inclusive society ensured that his legacy would guide South Africa's development for generations.

The adaptability of bold strategies is another key factor in their timelessness. Strategies must evolve to remain relevant, addressing new challenges while staying true to their core principles. The environmental movement provides a modern example of this adaptability. Initially focused on conservation, the movement has expanded to address climate change, renewable energy, and sustainable development. By adapting to emerging issues, environmental leaders have ensured that their strategies continue to drive progress.

For contemporary leaders, the timelessness of bold strategies is both an opportunity and a responsibility. It is an opportunity to create lasting impact by addressing fundamental challenges with creativity and vision. It is also a responsibility to ensure that strategies are ethical, inclusive, and sustainable, capable of serving future generations.

Practical applications of this mindset involve fostering a culture of reflection and learning. Leaders must regularly evaluate their strategies, seeking feedback and insights to refine their approach. This iterative process ensures that strategies remain dynamic and responsive to change.

Another important aspect is communication. Bold strategies often require collective effort, and leaders must articulate their vision in ways that inspire and unite others. The ability to convey purpose and urgency is essential for mobilizing support and sustaining momentum.

Ultimately, the timelessness of bold strategies lies in their ability to transcend individual achievements. Leaders like Alexander the Great, Martin Luther King Jr., and Nelson Mandela did not create their legacies in isolation; they inspired others to join their cause and carry their vision forward. Their strategies endured because they resonated with universal values, adapting to new contexts while remaining true to their essence.

For those who aspire to lead with impact, the lesson is clear: the most powerful strategies are those that endure. By grounding strategies in universal principles, embracing adaptability, and empowering others, leaders can shape a future that reflects their vision, ensuring that their contributions resonate across time and space.

CONCLUSION: THE POWER OF BOLD LEADERSHIP

As we conclude this journey through the strategies and stories of history's most innovative leaders, one truth stands out above all: leadership is an art as much as it is a science. It is shaped by vision, courage, resilience, and the ability to adapt. Bold leaders understand that their actions are not confined to the moments they inhabit but ripple forward in time, shaping the lives of countless others. This book has explored the principles and practices that empower leaders to create lasting impact, and now it is time to reflect on the essence of these lessons and what they mean for your journey.

At the heart of leadership lies the courage to dream big. From Alexander the Great's audacious conquests to Martin Luther King Jr.'s unwavering vision of equality, history teaches us that boldness begins with imagination. The leaders who left indelible marks on the world dared to articulate a vision that seemed unattainable, not because they were reckless, but because they understood the power of aspiration. They knew that great achievements are born not from small, cautious steps but from leaps of faith guided by a clear and compelling purpose.

But vision alone is not enough. Leadership demands action—the ability to transform ideas into reality through deliberate and decisive steps. This requires a deep understanding of timing, an appreciation for calculated risks, and the resilience to navigate setbacks. Leaders like Oprah Winfrey, who built a media empire through consistency and focus, or Nelson Mandela, who championed reconciliation despite immense challenges, exemplify the discipline required to bridge the gap between dreams and achievements.

Perhaps the most profound lesson from these leaders is the enduring value of adaptability. Change is the only constant, and those who lead effectively are those who embrace it. They view uncertainty not as an obstacle but as an opportunity to innovate, pivot, and grow. Whether it is Jeff Bezos transforming market disruptions into competitive advantages or Mahatma Gandhi adapting nonviolent resistance to the unique challenges of colonial rule, adaptability emerges as a cornerstone of lasting leadership.

Leadership is also inherently collaborative. No vision can flourish in isolation, and no leader can succeed without the support of others. This book has highlighted the importance of building networks of allies, fostering trust, and empowering teams to contribute their unique strengths. The stories of partnerships, like those of the Wright brothers or Franklin D. Roosevelt's co-alition-building, remind us that collective effort amplifies individual contributions, turning good ideas into transformative movements.

As we reflect on the timeless strategies explored in these chapters, it becomes clear that leadership is ultimately about legacy. The leaders who have truly shaped history are those who looked beyond their own lifetimes, embedding their values and principles into the systems, organizations, and people they touched. Walt Disney's creative empire, Jane Goodall's conservation efforts, and Gandhi's commitment to empowerment all serve as reminders that the most impactful leaders are those who plant seeds for the future.

So, what does this mean for you? Leadership is not confined to grand titles or global influence. It is a practice that begins with intention and manifests in everyday actions. You may not lead armies or build empires, but you have the power to influence, inspire, and create change within your own sphere. Whether it is mentoring a colleague, initiating a community project, or simply embodying the values you wish to see in the world, your leadership matters.

Take a moment to reflect on the lessons you've encountered in this book:

- **The Vision to Inspire**: Craft a vision that resonates not just with yourself but with those around you. Let it be bold, clear, and infused with purpose.

- **The Courage to Act**: Recognize that progress comes from action, even when the path is uncertain. Embrace calculated risks and learn from failure.

- **The Resilience to Endure**: Understand that

setbacks are inevitable but not insurmountable. Build the inner fortitude to persist through challenges.

- **The Wisdom to Collaborate**: Foster relationships, build teams, and create environments where others can thrive. Leadership is a shared journey.

- **The Commitment to Legacy**: Think beyond the immediate and consider how your actions today will shape the future. Invest in systems, mentorship, and values that endure.

As you move forward, consider this: leadership is not a destination but a journey. It is a continuous process of growth, learning, and refinement. Every decision you make, every challenge you face, and every opportunity you seize adds to the tapestry of your leadership story. And while the chapters of that story may not all be written yet, you hold the pen.

The leaders we have studied in this book were not without flaws. They were human, shaped by their circumstances and subject to their limitations. Yet, their willingness to strive for something greater—to contribute to a cause larger than themselves—defined their legacy. In the same way, your imperfections do not diminish your potential to lead with impact. What matters is your commitment to the principles and purpose that guide you.

As we close this chapter together, let us return to the idea of bold strategies. These are not strategies reserved for the exceptional few—they are tools available to anyone willing to think deeply, act courageously, and persevere. They are strategies that invite you to dream bigger, work smarter, and inspire others along the way.

History has shown us that the ripple effects of bold leadership extend far beyond what any one individual can predict. When you lead with vision, courage, and integrity, you contribute to a legacy that will outlast you—a legacy that shapes the world for the better.

This is your moment to step into that legacy, to apply these insights in your own life, and to lead with the same boldness and brilliance as the innovators who came before you. Whether your stage is global or local, your leadership matters. It has the power to inspire, transform, and endure.

So take what you've learned here and make it your own. Build your vision. Execute with purpose. Adapt with grace. Collaborate with generosity. And above all, lead with the confidence that your actions, however small, have the potential to leave a mark that lasts forever.

Go forth boldly. The future awaits.

ACKNOWLEDGEMENT

Every book is a collaborative effort, a convergence of inspiration, support, and shared wisdom. This one is no exception.

First and foremost, I want to express my deepest gratitude to the great leaders whose lives and legacies shaped the foundation of this book. Their stories, resilience, and bold strategies have provided lessons that transcend time, inspiring countless individuals, including myself.

To my family and friends, thank you for your unwavering encouragement and belief in my vision. Your patience and faith have been a source of strength during every late night and moment of reflection.

A heartfelt thanks to my editor and publishing team for their meticulous attention to detail and commitment to excellence. Your dedication transformed ideas into a polished and purposeful final product.

Finally, to the readers—your curiosity, ambition, and willingness to grow fuel the purpose behind these pages. This book was written for you, and I hope its lessons empower you to lead boldly and leave a lasting legacy of your own.

Thank you for being part of this journey. Together, we carry the torch forward.

ABOUT THE AUTHOR

Felix Grayson's journey into timeless wisdom began in childhood, captivated by the stories of philosophers, leaders, and visionaries who shaped the way we think and live. Growing up in a home filled with books, he spent countless hours exploring ideas that asked life's biggest questions—a curiosity that would later define his work.

After facing his own modern challenges—balancing ambition, uncertainty, and the search for meaning—Felix discovered that the wisdom of the past offers profound guidance for the present. This realization became the foundation for the *Stoned Philosopher* series: a collection dedicated to translating ancient insights into practical lessons for today's world.

Felix's writing is more than reflection—it's an invitation to dialogue with history's greatest minds. Through each book, he helps readers find clarity, resilience, and purpose in their own lives—one timeless idea at a time.

When not writing, Felix enjoys quiet contemplation, deep conversation, and exploring the endless pursuit of wisdom in everyday moments.

www.ingramcontent.com/pod-product-compliance
Lightning Source LLC
Chambersburg PA
CBHW021234130626
46554CB00004B/1491